WHEN REVIVAL COMES

Jack Taylor &
O. S. Hawkins

BROADMAN PRESS
Nashville, Tennessee

DEDICATION

To the fellowship of believers known as the First Baptist Church of Fort Lauderdale where "mercy drops round us are falling, but for the showers we plead" . . . And to anyone, anywhere hungering and thirsting for genuine revival

©Copyright 1980 • Broadman Press
All rights reserved
4262-26
ISBN: 0-8054-6226-0

All Scripture quotations are from the *New American Standard Bible.* Copyright © The Lockman Foundation, 1960, 1962, 1963, 1971, 1972, 1973, 1975. Used by permission.

Dewey Decimal Classification: 262.001
Subject heading: CHURCH RENEWAL
Library of Congress Catalog Card Number: 80-66956
Printed in the United States of America

PREFACE

We have been too long without a visitation from heaven. There is now no viable alternative to revival for America. It is revival or ruin and one or the other soon! I am not referring to religious excitement or rising fads in the ecclesiastical community. I am talking about a divine visitation from heaven of the kind that will turn the tide in America's rampage to ruin.

A long time ago I had to settle an issue in my ministry regarding revival. That question centered around whether it was something that could happen in conjunction with man's importunity in God's providence. I found out to my satisfaction that while God is sovereign, he invites us to pray for revival, promising us that when we do pray and humble ourselves, seeking his face and turning from our wicked ways, *then* he will hear from heaven, forgive our sins, and heal our lands. (2 Chron. 7:14) That settles it for me. This was all the theology of revival I needed to encourage me begin to pray until . . .

So I prayed and others prayed. We saw revival sweep through a local fellowship. More people were saved in a few months than had been saved in a dozen years previously. That was in 1970. There were similar visitations across the length and breadth of the land. There were some of the same features in those days that many of us had read about in previous awakenings.

Though much of significance has happened in the religious world that has been encouraging, the central features of a genuine spiritual awakening have been absent. Many churches have grown, Bible studies have magnetized the interest of thousands, and many hearts have been turned to the Lord. But with all of these, there has been little marked effect on the overall life-style of America. Crime continues to be rampant in our cities, juvenile delinquency and rebellion continue to rise, and indifference has a paralyzing grip on most of our churches.

The appalling corruption of our nation, the apparent closeness of His coming, and the absence of real commitment among most of the army of the Lord are all indications of the crying need for revival.

Here is a volume of expositions from the Book of Nehemiah which tells how revival can come—and what will happen when it comes. Principles drawn from this meaningful volume can be applied in any life and any situation with revival in mind.

It is my privilege to present the first chapter entitled, "Lord, Do It Again." It is also my privilege to add a postscript, an epilogue, at the end.

There are many churches where conditions are strangely similar to historical descriptions of revival. They seem to be in the early stages of real awakening. The First Baptist Church of Fort Lauderdale, Florida, is one of these. O. S. Hawkins is the young pastor of this exciting church. Remarkably anointed by the Spirit of God, this young pastor, yet in his early thirties, is being used of God to spark awakening wherever he preaches.

Your heart will warm to these expositions from God's Word. I commend this volume to you with prayers for revival in your life and ministry.

JACK R. TAYLOR, President
Dimensions in Christian Living
Fort Worth, Texas

INTRODUCTION

It was a hot, humid summer evening during my grammar school days. A big tent had been erected in our neighborhood. Walking home from a sandlot ball game, my friends and I decided to see what was happening inside. One of the boys went on home, claiming we would get scared due to the fact that the people acted "spooky." He was right. They did and we were!

Never had I seen anything in my young years like the spectacle that night. People yelled and screamed. Some danced around in a daze. Others got down in the sawdust aisles and rolled in ecstasy. Many spoke in a "language" I had never heard. Being somewhat frightened by it all we left rather hurriedly. As we walked across the vacant lot I looked at the sign out front. Written in flaming red letters across a white-washed "four by eight" plywood sheet was the word—REVIVAL! What an impression that made on my young life. It was the first time I had seen or heard of the word, *revival.* And for the next several years I associated revival with what I saw and heard that sultry summer evening.

I am becoming convinced that the word revival is one of the most misunderstood words in our Christian vocabulary. It means so many different things to so many different people. As we journey together through these pages in quest of revival, it is of extreme importance that we all embark from the same launching pad. Let me come up with a definition.

Revival is, as I heard Stephen Olford express it, "that strange and sovereign work of God in which he visits his own people, restoring, reanimating, and releasing them into the fullness of his blessing."

What you are about to read has been born and cradled in prayer. We desire that you will be supernaturally moved to pray and believe God for a mighty moving of the Holy Spirit through our churches and land.

With excitement let's discover what happens . . . *when revival comes!*

O. S. HAWKINS, Pastor
First Baptist Church
Fort Lauderdale, Florida

Authors' Note:

At the beginning of each chapter there is a brief, personal story. Each relates a true-life experience from within the context of a geninue revival atmosphere. Because every person, in reality, is a microcosm of the larger group to which they belong, it is both interesting and productive to view the individual happenings. May God bless these to your enjoyment.

Table of Contents

GOD BRINGS THE MISSION FIELD

When God chooses to do a sovereign work of revival it seems that regardless of where the church is located, he literally brings the mission field to its door. The First Baptist Church of Fort Lauderdale is located only a few miles from where ships of many nations come to dock. Sailors from around the world are being saved and are becoming missionaries in their world.

During the moving of God in revival the aircraft carrier *Nimitz* was docked at Fort Lauderdale. Several sailors came to know Jesus through the ministry of the witnesses from the church. Those sailors returned to their ship and began Bible studies. It was not long before the ship was dispatched to a troubled spot in the world. There it stood, a veritable, floating mission station with witnesses in its mammoth community—who had found Christ in revival.

On another occasion a group of pastors from Australia visited the church to study its growth and discover principles which would help grow churches in "the land down under." I discussed with them the matter of praying for the lost. After they returned to their country some of them became serious about putting into action the principles they had learned. One of them wrote back that when his people began praying for the lost like I had mentioned, his own church began to experience revival. As a result people were being saved in all services of the church.

When God starts a fire he wants it to spread. Genuine revival cannot continue to be localized. God will make sure that it catches on in other places. Businesses are transferring their employees to other places, and lives ignited by revival are being used to spark revival fires elsewhere.

This is God's method of accomplishment . . . *when revival comes!*

Chapter 1

LORD, DO IT AGAIN!

Lord, Do It Again!

Stories of fresh breathings of God's power in history at the darkest times in mankind's existence form a most thrilling commentary. There were ages past when it seemed that all hope for morality and decency were forever gone.

Then revival came, often suddenly, and with it a sudden reversal of trends, removing of foul ideologies, and revitalization of moral standards. I offer for your observation a brief look at several of the more notable spiritual awakenings in history. I offer these with the prayer that in these days of illicit sex and scandal, riot and revolution, indifference and boredom there might be raised to God a fresh barrage of prayers from revival in these closing days of century twenty.

Lord, as you have in times past breathed upon the fallen world with a fresh breath of your power . . . do it again! Do it again!

Let's gaze at some of those days and discover God's patterns of revival for our day.

THE PURITAN REVIVAL

This revival began, as all revivals do, around the Word of God and prayer Through the labors of William Tyndale, the Book of God was given to the people in their own tongue. When the Bible first appeared in English form, there were only six copies of it. These were set up in the nave of an edifice in London, England.

Day after day crowds flocked in to hear the reading of the Bible. Readers were in great demand. Soon the scene of people standing for hours was repeated across the land in many churches. It was not long before the Bible in the form of the small Geneva Version was sent into the homes of the people.

The faithful Book began to do its work, indicting careless, unfeeling shepherds and sending them to their knees, as they repented of sin and interceded in behalf of their cold, lifeless churches. Men and women began to be converted everywhere. These converts were marked at once as peculiar people. No wonder they appeared to their neighbors as inhabitants of another sphere. Folks tried to find a name for them, and as often happened before and since, the name they were given stayed with them. They were called Puritans!

THE NEW ENGLAND REVIVAL AND THE GREAT AWAKENING

This revival in its beginning stages seemed to center around a young preacher by the name of Jonathan Edwards. Brilliant of mind and consumed with a passsion to know God, this man was to be used of God to ignite the fires of revival as few men in history. He ministered in a community where sin was rampant with all moral values seemingly thrown to the wind. He faithfully preached and fervently prayed. Devoid of pulpit beauty as such, he read his sermons with a voice that was weak. Yet these sermons thus delivered held people spellbound and caused some to grasp the seats in front of them lest they should fall into the hell Edwards so vividly described.

It seemed to happen all of a sudden (we will see that phrase again). A young woman, a great sinner in the community, was gloriously saved. She was immediately a new creature. News of her conversion spread like wildfire, and with it the conviction of the Spirit in hearts that heard about it. The city (Northampton) was literally filled with the conscious awareness of the presence of God.

In the early months of 1735 people pressed into the church daily to worship God and pray. The Bible came alive. It seemed to thousands that it was a new Book. Texts that had been read a thousand times appeared with such novel interest that old saints were tempted to think they had never seen them before.

Taverns were emptied. In the streets at all hours of the day and night, people paused to speak of the beauty and never-ending love of Christ. The result of the revival was that almost the whole adult population of the town was added to the church. Ministers came from other places to view revival and went back to carry word and power of this revival to their congregations.

REVIVAL UNDER WESLEY

In 1738 John Wesley entered upon his new life. He cast himself on Christ and ceased from weary, hopeless struggling, finding precious the unutterable peace of God. He began to preach with whole-hearted conviction, and such were the results that many churches closed their doors to his ministry.

Many a time after a particularly disturbing and convicting message he would hear these words, "Sir, you cannot preach here again!" But the common people heard him gladly and prayed with him in earnestness for revival.

George Whitefield had been drawn into the group which included John and Charles Wesley, and was to be mightily used in the awakening. So great was the conviction that came as a result of Whitefield's preaching that he was accused of driving people mad.

One day he was preaching in a full building and saw a sight which chilled his soul. He looked out through the open door to see thousands of disappointed persons who could not get through to hear the message of salvation. The thought came that he should preach in the open area outside. When the thought was shared with his brethen they condemned it as fanatical. He persisted, however, and before long most churches in the area were closed to him.

He then went to the field and found his pulpit on the green hillsides. On Saturday afternoon, February 17, 1739, he took his stand on a little green hill in a wild mining region. To his amazement (and theirs) 200 people gathered to hear him. He continued day after day until the crowds filled the hedges and climbed the trees to hear him . . . more than 20,000 in one service. In that service, as he preached Whitefield saw a moving sight. Tears were plowing white furrows down dirty faces of miners fresh from the mines, their faces drenched by penitential waters. Dirty hearts were cleansed by the precious blood of Christ.

I pray, "Lord, as you did it in the Puritan days, as you did it in Edwards's day and Wesley's day, and Whitefield's day . . .DO IT AGAIN! DO IT AGAIN!"

REVIVAL UNDER BRAINERD

By most standards we should never have heard the name of David Brainerd.

He literally burnt out his life, pouring it out
in early sacrifice. He might have held a
wealthy pastorate in New England but
chose instead to minister to a people who
seemed to be in no one's care. He spent
his brief life in journeyings among the
American Indians, covering more than
3,000 miles through trackless forests, over
dangerous mountains, in driving rains,
and freezing cold.

His strength ebbed, and as it did, his
compassion and zeal for the lost seemed
to grow. Whole nights were spent in the
dark woods, his clothes drenched with the
sweat of his travail. On one particular
evening God so mightily dealt with him
that suddenly (there is the word again) the
Spirit was poured out on the whole region
of Susquehanna.

As God moved it was nothing for men
and women from all sides to accost him,
grabbing the bridle of his horse, and to
plead with him to tell how they might be
saved. In great, glad wonder he preached
to them the good tidings of salvation in
Christ.

Men fell at his feet in anguish of soul,
hard men who could bear the most acute
torture without flinching. But now they
cried unashamedly, "Have mercy on
me!" The woods were filled with the

sounds of mourning. A passion for righteousness possessed the new converts. Victims of strong drink were delivered at once. The light spread throughout the dark region. In 1747 David Brainerd breathed the last breath of a most effective life, though the span of his life was far less than half the seventy years allotted for man.

As I ponder this one, solitary life and the mark God made with it on those bleak days of history, I am moved to pray, "Lord, as you did it under Brainerd . . . DO IT AGAIN! DO IT AGAIN!"

REVIVAL UNDER FINNEY

As the eighteenth century came to a close, the churches of America in the main were in a sickly state. False doctrine abounded. Dreary apathy prevailed. But in the midst of the national darkness, God was active in preparing an instrument.

The instrument, rough and rebellious at first, at last began to bend to the divine pull. It was then that Charles Grandison Finney, a young skeptic, suddenly (that word again) fell on his knees and gave his life to the God whose very existence he had previously doubted. Another experience in a wooded area seemed to be his enduement with power from on high, and he literally came out of the woods preaching the Gospel.

The news of his dramatic conversion spread far and wide. His ministry was to continue for a half a century, and the dominant theme was *revival!* He preached a total gospel packed with meat for the believer's growth and conviction to encourage the sinner to turn from the error of his ways. Hell was no myth but a stern reality from which he called all men to flee. Prayer to him was a passion. If there was a season when the power of God upon him seemed to be less than before, he would retreat for a time of fasting and prayer until he was anointed by God with "fresh oil" for a mighty ministry. He refused to minister without the hand of God upon him.

Wherever he preached church members confessed that they had never known the grace of God in salvation and gladly experienced saving grace. At a certain place, an immaculate, well-dressed lady was the first to answer the altar call. An exemplary church member, she confessed that her whole experience had been a falsehood.

She came with the humility of a child and was saved immediately!

On another occasion he was asked to preach at a place which was often called "little Sodom" because of its open, blatant wickedness. He preached to a fearful-looking crowd. Before he was through, this great crowd of wicked men and women fell, almost to the last one, on their knees and cried in conviction for heavenly mercy. The meeting continued until the next morning.

Few men in his day were marked by the power of God upon their lives as was Charles Finney. On one occasion, so the account goes, he was visiting a factory at the invitation of the factory owner. A lady on an assembly line looked sneeringly at the visiting preacher. His gaze met hers, and immediately she fell under conviction. The reaction swept through the factory, and business was suspended in favor of revival.

The spirit of revival also spread through whole regions. In one mining region alone, over 5,000 souls were converted without a single minister being settled in the whole area. Dr. Lyman Beecher said of the awakening, "This is the greatest work of God and the greatest revival of religion that the world has ever seen in such a short time." One hundred thousand were reported as having connected themselves with the church in a short period.

As I read and ponder these reports, my prayer is, "Lord, do it again! Do it again!"

And there have been many other sweeping revivals which have been reported in documented history books. There were revivals in Scotland, the Hebrides, Wales, and in our own century the great revival that swept North China. But I want to share with you some little-known observations regarding the most intriguing (for me) of all the awakenings.

THE REVIVAL OF 1857

The 1850s found America in a sad and sickened state. There was great luxury on the part of few and great poverty on the part of many. Crime rates soared. Violence was common. City streets were unsafe. Free love was espoused, and the home seemed to be on the verge of collapse. Economic instability haunted the nation, and unemployment raged out of control. Corruption and injustice shamelessly walked hand in hand in high places.

Racial division (the slavery question) separated family and friends. Many wondered if "the land of the free and the home of the brave" was not writing the last chapter of its history.

In 1857, perhaps given urgency by the severe national crisis which touched every area of life, God's people began to become serious about prayer for revival. There was a revival of prayer. This revival is often referred to as "The Prayer Revival." There was first a revival of prayer, not casual, passive prayer but vital, importunate prayer. In most revivals, a single man is particularly used and is thus associated with the revival. This revival was an exception. This may have been one of the reasons why the exact time and place of its beginning is not certain. The wonderful thing is this . . . in answer to the church's desperate cry, ascending from all parts of the land, the Spirit of God in a quiet way at first, and then suddenly (again!) throughout the length and breadth of the land, renewed the church's life, and wakened in the community around it a deep thirst for God.

Many meetings are worthy of note. One is the prayer meeting which later became famous under the name of "The Fulton

Street Prayer Meeting." Jeremiah Lamphier was a preacher in New York. He had a tremendous burden for revival. He called on a few Christians to meet with him at a location on Fulton Street for a prayer meeting in behalf of revival. He arrived at the appointed place on September 23, 1857. He was later joined by five others.

This inauspicious meeting was the beginning of a mighty prayer meeting from which dozens like it were launched across the country. Soon businessmen were closing their businesses and meeting in prayer meetings to beseech God in behalf of their beloved country. The prayer meetings were simply that and no more. Requests were read, and prevailing prayer followed. Many were converted in the prayer meetings themselves.

Throughout the land, divine fire broke out, and white-haired penitents knelt with little children to receive Christ. Whole families of Jews were converted to their true Messiah. Deaf mutes were reached with the glad tidings of salvation and, though their tongues were still, their faces shone with such brightness that they, without words, became effective messengers of the Gospel. The most hardened infidels were melted, some being led to

Christ by the testimonies of little children.

Some of the most amazing aspects of this revival are recorded in only a few little-known accounts. The blessings of this atmospheric visitation was not confined to land. The Spirit of God literally moved upon the face of the waters. A multitude of seamen saw the light while yet at sea. Ships, as they drew near to land, seemed to come within the zone of heavenly influence.

Vessel after vessel arrived at land with the same tale of a mysterious conviction breaking out among the crewmen, followed by dramatic conversions to Christ. On one such vessel a captain and an entire crew of thirty men found Christ at sea and entered the harbor with rejoicing. Perhaps the most striking awakening took place on a battleship.

The *North Carolina* (a battleship) lay in New York harbor. Her complement was about a thousand men. On board there were four men who discovered their spiritual kinship and agreed to meet together for prayer. They were given permission to use a remote part of the ship far below the water line for their meeting. They represented three denominations. One was a Presbyterian, one was an

Episcopalian, and two were Baptists.

One evening as they met for prayer in the light of a tiny lamp, the Spirit of God suddenly (!!) so filled their hearts that they burst forth in joyous song. The sweet strain of their song rose to the deck above. Merry-making sailors were astonished and came running down. They came to mock, but the mighty power of God had been liberated by rejoicing faith. That power gripped them with such force that their laughs of ridicule were changed to cries of repentance, and they were smitten on the spot. Thus a great work began deep within that ship.

Night after night as prayer meetings were held, sailors were converted. They were forced to send ashore for help in counseling the inquirers. The old battleship soon became a veritable house of God, a floating, spiritual battle station, spreading the witness of the awakening everywhere!

It is estimated that during the months of the revival's greatest intensity, no less than 50,000 persons a week were swept into the kingdom of God. Conservative estimates claimed that more than a million people met Jesus Christ as Savior in less than a twelve-month span.

Lord, do it again! Do it again!

THE REVIVAL OF
THE NINETEEN EIGHTIES???

Is it not due time again? When the heart of the church in many quarters has turned to stone; the pulpit, a dispensary of human philosophies; our educational systems, citadels of unprincipled corruption, shameless atheism, and blatant humanism . . . is it not time again to pray, Lord, do it again as in times of old? Is it not time for the people of God to barrage heaven with cries for revival? When the Bible has been laid aside as error-filled and rated with worn-out books of antiquity, and humanistic philosophies are being taught instead, is not our only hope genuine revival?

When old-fashioned evangelistic methods, once openly espoused, are condemned as crude and old-fashioned, and the altar call after hell-fire preaching is called a fear tactic, is it not time to cry to God for a return to Him?

When I see our nation sinking rapidly into the quicksands of immorality and insensitivity, with a seeming inability to call itself to arms, I say, "Lord, visit us again with your sovereign power!" When from television, newspapers, and other public media I hear the raucous cries of a thousand voices calling my children and yours to life-styles of godlessness, I am moved to pray, "Lord, do it again! Revive us again that thy people may rejoice in thee."

When I see churches settling down to tolerate comfortably a declining civilization and adjusting their demands to accommodate indifference, I know it is time for real revival. Nothing else will do!

When I see Christians pitifully struggling with half-hearted zeal to regain their first love, and seeking to nurse a quiet desperation within their breasts, I know revival is the only answer.

When I can imagine that I hear the cries of the Savior who wept over Jerusalem, weeping over this sin-cursed earth, I am moved to pray with Isaiah of old as he cried:

Oh, that thou wouldst rend the heavens and come down (Isa. 64:1).

It is with this in mind that these expositions are presented. May God breathe upon them to your heart with the result being a fresh appetite for revival, personal and corporate.

ANGEL UNAWARE

Do not forget to entertain strangers, for by doing, some people have entertained angels unaware (Heb. 13:1).

He was an unlikely prospect, to say the least, but without a doubt was the most important visitor of the week. With worn, out-of-date clothes, unkept hair, and unshaven face, he came to the morning service.

He happened to sit down by a couple who had been recently converted to Christ. They made him feel welcome and literally wrapped him in arms of Christian love. During the invitation he came forward as an inquirer regarding this new life about which I had preached.

A counselor guided him to the counseling room where he trusted Christ as his Savior. Before I left the church that afternoon the old man said, "Sir, I just ate my first meal in four days. A man from the church took me to lunch. Oh sir, I feel so happy and bubbly on the inside."

He then made a strange request. He asked if there were an old broom anywhere around the church. He then spent the afternoon sweeping off the sidewalks and porches of the church where he had met Christ a few hours before.

Before he left that evening he gave an offering—the only thing he had to his name, a battered old flashlight. He disappeared as quickly as he had appeared.

More often than we realize do we entertain angels unaware . . . *when revival comes!*

Chapter 2

WHEN REVIVAL COMES

CHAPTER 2
When Revival Comes

(Nehemiah 1:1-11)

Revival comes when we:

I. RECOGNIZE ITS DEMAND (1-3)

A. Discouragement Leads to Distress (3)— "people in great distress"

B. Distress Lends Itself to Dishonor (3)—"people are reproach"

C. Dishonor Leaves Us Defenseless (3)—"walls broken; gates burned"

II. RESPOND IN DESPERATION (4)

A. Contemplation—"sat down"

B. Compassion—"wept"

C. Concern—"mourned for days"

D. Concentration—"fasted"

E. Communion—"prayed before God of Heaven"

III. REQUEST A DELIVERANCE (5-11)

A. Confession (5-7)

B. Consecration (6)

C. Conditions (8-9)

D. Claim (10-11)

When Revival Comes

*The words of Nehemiah the son of
Hacaliah. Now it happened in the
month Chislev, in the twentieth year,
while I was in Susa the capitol, that
Hanani, one of my brothers, and
some men from Judah came; and
asked them concerning the Jews
who had escaped and had survived
the captivity, and about Jerusalem.
And they said to me, "The remnant
there in the province who survived
the captivity are in distress and
reproach, and the wall of Jerusalem
is broken down and its gates are
burned with fire." Now it came
about when I heard these words, I
sat down and wept and mourned
for days; and I was fasting and
praying before the God of heaven.
And I said, "I beseech Thee, O Lord*

God of heaven, the great and awesome God, who preserves the covenant and loving kindness for those who love Him and keep His commandments, let Thine ear now be attentive and Thine eyes open to hear the prayer of Thy servant which I am praying before Thee now, day and night, on behalf of the sons of Israel Thy servants, confessing the sins of the sons of Israel which we have sinned . . . "We have acted very corruptly against Thee and have not kept the commandments, nor the statutes, nor the ordinances which Thou didst command Thy servant Moses. "Remember the word which Thou didst command Thy servant Moses, saying, "If you are unfaithful I will scatter you among the peoples; but if you return to me and keep My commandments and do them, though those of you who have been scattered were in the most remote part of the heavens, I will gather them from there and will bring them to the place where I have chosen to cause My name to dwell; and they are Thy servants and Thy people whom Thou didst redeem by Thy great power and by Thy strong hand. O Lord, I beseech Thee, may Thine ear be attentive to the prayer of Thy servant and the prayers of Thy servants who delight to revere Thy name, and make Thy servant successful today, and grant him compassion before this man." Now I was the cupbearer to the king (Neh. 1:1-11).

What is our greatest need today? Investors are claiming it is financial security. Insurance salesmen are insisting our greatest need is adequate retirement benefits and protection. Social workers are stressing it is feeding and clothing the hungry and poor. Educators tell us our greatest need is more learning. Still others contend that our greatest need is to squelch Communist infiltration.

Ask fifty people that question and most likely you will receive fifty different answers! However, I am convinced our greatest need today is *revival,* the kind of revival that results in repentance, restitution, reunited homes, reunion, transformed life-styles, and love, love, love! Yes, what we need more than anything is revival. What our nation needs is revival. What our churches need is revival. What

our homes need is revival. We need
revival!

When does *revival come?* The answer to
this all-important question is found in
Chapter one of Nehemiah 1. Here is *one* of
the most amazing and revealing chapters
in the Word of God. In order to understand
its developments in their fullness, we must
be familiar with the circumstances which
precede and surround its happenings.

The Jewish people had been taken into
the Babylonian captivity and had been
captive to Babylon for 70 years. Then, in
530 BC the armies of Persia broke the
Babylonian supremacy, and the King of
Persia released the Jewish remnant and
encouraged them to return to Jerusalem.

At that time 50,000 Israelites did return
and began immediately to reconstruct the
demolished Temple. They soon became
discouraged by opposition from the people who had settled there during the captivity. They abandoned their task with only
the foundation having been rebuilt. A few
years later, Haggai and Zechariah appeared on the scene, pointed out the people's neglect, and challenged them to
finish the job. This they did twenty years
after their return.

Sixty more years passed, and under

Ezra's leadership more of the remnant returned to Jerusalem. Although the Temple had been rebuilt, the walls of the city were in shambles and the gates burned. So for ninety years after the first Jews returned, the people of God lived in affliction and shame in a city with broken walls and burned gates.

It was then that God prepared Nehemiah and called him into service during the rebuilding of the walls of Jerusalem. It was his task to leave the security of his home and be the agent of God in bringing revival to his people by rebuilding the walls.

Friend, I fear there are some broken-down walls around our lives that desperately need to be rebuilt! I am going to deal with rebuilding of these walls in the following, and especially in this chapter.

We need a revival! When does revival come? Revival comes, first of all, when we:

RECOGNIZE ITS DEMAND

The words of Nehemiah the son of Hacaliah. Now it happened in the month Chislev, in the twentieth year, while I was in Susa the capitol, that

> Hanani, one of my brothers, and some men from Judah came; and I asked them concerning the Jews who had escaped and had survived the captivity, and about Jerusalem. And they said to me, "The remnant there in the province who survived the captivity are in great distress and reproach, and the wall of Jerusalem is broken down and its gates are burned with fire" (1:1-3).

Revival never comes to any person until he realizes the dire need of it. Nehemiah was busy at his job of being cupbearer to the king. Everything was going on as usual. He was caught up in the midst of a busy routine. And then . . . from his visiting kinsmen the news came of the need of revival in Jerusalem.

The reason many of us see no need for revival is because we are so busy with our weekly routine that we have almost become spiritually blind and deaf. Many of us are so busy doing church work and other good things that we are deaf to the call of revival.

What was the report that Nehemiah received concerning the situation in Jerusalem? The reporters relayed this information to Nehemiah—"the people were in distress, the people were a reproach to God because of their neglect, the walls were broken down, and the gates were burned!" Upon hearing this report, Nehemiah also heard the call of God to be the rebuilder of those broken walls. It is important to note that he did not recognize the need for revival, for the walls to be rebuilt, until he heard of them being in ruins. The outlook was far from bright. But such an outlook is as necessary to revival as pain is to medical attention. The sensing of pain, as agonizing as it often is, is often the beginning of a chain reaction that climaxes in healing. Such was the case with Nehemiah.

Discouragement Leads to Distress

There was no movement to remedy the sad situation back in the homeland until the sad and discouraging report came to the ears of Nehemiah. It was the discouragement which led to distress.

The report is the same for us today! These are the same conditions which demand revival in our lives now! For one thing, the people of God are in distress. That is, God's people are not bound together in unity as they ought to be. Also, we find that many of God's people today are a reproach to him just as the Israelites were in the day of Nehemiah. Too many of God's people today are compromising with the world, going where the world goes, saying what the world says, living like the world lives, talking like the world talks, and acting like the world acts!

Distress Lends Itself to Dishonor

The whole situation in Jerusalem was a reproach to God. The people who had come back to the land were seeking to become comfortable in conditions unpleasing to God.

When we try to live for God on the one hand and the world on the other, we are a reproach to him, and the world looks on at our phoniness and wants no part of it. We must see revival in our day because of the reproach of so many of God's people to his Holy Name.

Dishonor Leaves Us Defenseless

More serious than all other conditions were those which found the walls broken down and the gates burned with fire. The

Jews were virtually defenseless. This meant that they were prey to every nation around them. They could pursue no purpose. They could make no plans. There could be no unity.

Today we have spiritual walls that have been broken down. Walls of Bible study, walls of family worship, wall of interpersonal relationships, walls of morality, walls of holiness, walls of commitment that need to be rebuilt. Some of our walls are in ruins and demand revival. The final condition today which demands revival is the fact that our gates are burned. The gates are burned—so, we are vulnerable to the enemy. There is nothing in many lives to keep Satan and his attack away. By our neglect and our compromise we have burned the gates, and we are vulnerable to the enemy and his attack.

Do you see the condition we are in? Do you recognize the demand for revival? If not, this is probably your major problem. We will never see revival until, first of all, we recognize its demand. Nehemiah was called to rebuild the walls, but first he had to weep over the ruins. I wonder, do we really see the ruin in which our walls lie? Oh, we need revival. When does revival come? When we recognize its demand.

And secondly, when we:

RESPOND IN DESPERATION

"Now it came about when I heard these words, I sat down and wept and mourned for days; for I was fasting and praying before the God of Heaven" (1:4).

Have you recognized the demand for revival? Have you seen the conditions which demand it in your own life? Then, what will you do about it? It is not enough just to recognize its demand—revival comes when we respond in desperation.

A look at what Nehemiah did at this point will give us a valuable hint at the kind of attitude which must precede revival. Look at what Nehemiah did . . . he sat down, he wept, he mourned for days, he fasted, and he prayed before the God of heaven.

Contemplation

It is very important to note that first of all, he sat down. He took time to concentrate and evaluate. He sought the face of God. He was willing to be the means of revival.

How long has it been since you recognized the demand for revival and stopped long enough to sit down and reflect and evaluate on your relationship to Jesus? Would you be willing to say, "I want to be the means of revival coming to my heart, my home, my church, my life"?

Too much cannot be said about the indispensability of such a person as Nehemiah to revival. The price begins to be paid by someone. That someone must be willing to choose revival above all other pursuits, abandoning all for this "pearl of great price." A young man in Wales by the name of Evan Roberts counted that cost in the early part of this century, and the result was a mighty spiritual awakening. It all began, as with Nehemiah, with contemplation.

Compassion

In the process of spiritual concern, deep compassion can only follow serious contemplation. If we do not take time for contemplation which reveals the seriousness of the situation, there is generally no compassion. Nehemiah sat down, and then the Bible tells us that he *wept*. He thought about the distress, the reproach of the people, the broken walls, the burned gates, the need for revival, and those conditions broke his heart and he wept, and he wept, and he wept! He was desperate.

How long has it been since you shed tears over conditions in your life that demand revival? Have you been a reproach to God or a stumbling block to others? Perhaps your walls need rebuilding, your gates are burned, and the enemy has made his attack. Does it matter to you? Where are our tears?

Concern

This weeping of Nehemiah was not a momentary fit of compassion. This was no light emotional outburst. One may weep for a moment over something as light as a silly, little story, but when one mourns for days, compassion has doubtlessly become genuine concern. Not only did Nehemiah sit down and weep, but he also *mourned* for days. He mourned and mourned. He was burdened, deeply burdened, over the neglect and indifference of the people of God. Does it bother you? Your indifference? The indifference of others? The way we react so often with lovelessness? How long has it been since you sat down, wept, and mourned for days?

Concentration

There is a certain exclusiveness about the burden which brings revival. All other pursuits must be abandoned. I think Nehemiah was forced to fast because of the intensity of his great burden for his homeland.

The Scriptures simply state that Nehemiah *fasted*. This seems to be a lost word in our Christian vocabulary. Nehemiah went without food so he could constantly have the matter before him in prayer. Every hunger pain reminded him of the reason for his fast. He continued to pound the throne of Heaven with his request for revival. Have you ever been so burdened over a matter that you fasted? Many in the Bible fasted. David, Nehemiah, Daniel, our Lord, and multiplied scores of others. In fact, Jesus said, "Some things only come by prayer and fasting." You see, Nehemiah meant business with God. He was desperate to see revival.

Communion

Finally, verse 4 tells us that *he prayed before the God of heaven*. After all, this is the delivery room of revival. This is where the labor pains of godly concern result in the birth of revival. It can happen in no other manner.

For Nehemiah praying was warfare! He was desperate. He agonized! He wept! He mourned! He fasted! He prayed . . . for days he prayed! Is it any wonder that revival came? I am afraid that we do not hear much of that kind of praying these days.

Most of our praying is so superficial . . . "Lord, bless this," or, "Lord, bless that . . . Lord, save old John Doe . . . Lord, bless the people who are ill . . . Lord, do this, Lord do that . . . if it be thy will." You know, we always add that last phrase as an escape clause so God won't get trapped! Friend, how long has it been since you have prayed before the God of heaven for days? Real prayer involves battle. Real prayer is rooted in the promises of God! Real prayer brings revival!

Our problem today is not so much that we do not recognize the demand for revival. Our real problem lies in the way we respond. Most of us just limp along forever trying to be satisfied with the carnal life. It is no wonder so many live a life of continual defeat with little or no victory.

Nehemiah responded in desperation. He sat down, wept, mourned for days, fasted, and prayed before the God of heaven! He would not be satisfied with anything less than revival. *Friend, if you can do without revival—you will!* More than anything, we need to come to the point of dissatisfaction and desperation.

We need a revival. We need the kind of revival where the Holy Spirit has the freedom to sweep over us in conviction. We need the kind of revival where God's people repent of sin and open their lives to the Lord Jesus. When will revival come? It will come only when we recognize its demand, respond in desperation, and finally:

REQUEST A DELIVERANCE

And I said, "I beseech Thee, O Lord God of heaven, the great and awesome God, who preserves the covenant and lovingkindness for those who love Him and keep His commandments, let Thine ear now be attentive and Thine eyes open to hear the prayer of Thy servant which I am praying before Thee now, day and night, on behalf of the sons of Israel Thy servants, confessing the sins of the sons of Israel which we have sinned against Thee; I and my father's house have sinned. "We have acted very corruptly against Thee and have not kept the commandments, nor the ordinances which Thou didst command Thy servant Moses. Remember the word which Thou didst command Thy servant Moses saying, 'If you are unfaithful I will scatter you among the peoples; but if you return to Me and keep my commandments and do them, though those of you who have been scattered were in the most remote part of the heavens, I will gather them from there and will bring them to the place where I have chosen to cause My name to dwell.' "And they are thy servants . . . O Lord, I beseech Thee, may Thine ear be attentive to the prayer of Thy servant and the prayer of Thy servants who delight to revere Thy name, and make Thy servant successful today, and grant him compassion before this man" (1:5-11).

You can recognize its demand and you can respond in desperation, but it is not until you "beseech the Lord God of heaven" and request a deliverance that revival comes!

Confession

Nehemiah's request involved *confession* (1:5-7). Nehemiah said, "We have sinned." He was specific in confessing his sin. He didn't say, "We made a mistake." Nor did he say, "If we have sinned." He cried, "We have sinned, I have sinned!" How long has it been since you got hold of the ear of God and said, " I have sinned"? Be serious. Think about it a moment. How long has it been? It is no wonder we are not in revival. Revival will never come until we take this step of confession.

If we confess our sins, He is faithful and righteous to forgive us our sins, and to cleanse us from all unrighteousness (1 John 1:9).

Consecration

Secondly, Nehemiah's request involved *consecration* (1:6). Nehemiah was consecrated to God. He beseeched him "day and night'' for four months (2:1) Nehemiah meant business with God. He reminds us of Jacob wrestling with the angel through the night, saying, ''I will not let you go until you bless me.'' What about you? Is there any consecration in your life? Do you mean business with God? Are you ready to say to him, ''I will not let you go until you bless me''?

Conditions

Next, we see that revival comes when we understand that it is conditional . . . (1:8-9). It is conditional upon repentance! ''If you return to me . . .'' (1:9). In a very real sense, revival is not a miracle. It is simply the direct response of God to conditions met by his people. ''*If* my people which are called by my name humble themselves and pray and seek my face and turn from their wicked ways, *then* I will hear from heaven, will forgive their sin, and heal their land'' (2 Chron. 7:14).

God is waiting, willing, and longing to send revival to anyone that will repent. We must repent. We cannot be trusted with a thing as holy as revival and have the devil in our lives. We cannot do it! Revival is conditional upon repentance, and this chapter is an urgent appeal for us to turn from our sin to serve the living Lord Jesus.

Claim

Finally, we see that an important part of this request for deliverance is in claiming the promises of God (1:10-11). Nehemiah believed God and expected him to do what he said he would do! He claimed his promises by faith! I suppose one of the things we must do today more than ever is simply to take God at his Word . . . We need to realize that he longs to see us in revival. He longs to see us conformed to his image. He longs to see us as the representative, visible part of the body of Christ in our world today. He longs to see us live holy lives before him. He longs to see us not be conformed to the world but be transformed by his power.

Oh, we need a revival! When does revival come? Revival comes only after we recognize its demand, respond in desperation, and then request a deliverance.

But wait a minute! I have left off the last sentence in the chapter. I have left it off . . . until now! Nehemiah adds, seemingly out of context, "Now I was the cupbearer to the king" (1:11). Do you see the depth and importance of that statement? Nehemiah was the trusted confidant of the king—his cupbearer. He tasted everything before the king tasted it to make certain that the king was not being poisoned. He was the close and continual companion of the king. He had a high salary. He was fixed for life. He had a civil-service job, along with good retirement benefits.

"But you see," he said, "my people are in reproach and when people see the walls and gates they will say, 'what a poor God you have,' so I must get involved, whatever the cost!" He was willing to abandon what he had and be identified with the cause of God! He abandoned prestige. He abandoned power. He abandoned popularity. He abandoned prosperity. He abandoned pride. He gave it all up to be the agent of revival!

Now let me ask you—would you be willing to say, "I do not care what the cost, I want to see revival"? "I do not care what people say. I want to see revival. It does not matter if I am not the center of everyone's attention. I want to see revival. It does not matter if it costs me my pride or my prestige. I want to be an agent of the Holy Spirit in revival. My meat is to do the will of him who sent me while there is time." Friend, then and only then is . . . when revival comes!

I dare you to be that man, that woman, that boy, that girl. Are you willing? Are you willing to be made willing? Are you willing to say, "Lord, pursue me, chase me down, convict me of my sin, and draw me to be the agent of revival"? Often the Lord touches us at our strong points. He may touch an area of your pride and say, "Throw it down."

> Send a revival, O Christ, my Lord,
> Let it go over the land and sea,
> Send it according to thy dear Word,
> And let it begin in me.*

We need a revival! *You* could be the key! Recognize its demand. Respond in desperation. And go on, request a deliverance!

A REVERSAL OF PRIORITIES

Don was both a successful plastic surgeon and a businessman. Often as he drove by the church on the downtown corner he cast an eye toward it and thought, *What a waste of premium real estate space.* He had planned and lived his life up until then without regard for God. He had made it on his own and had done quite well. Why should there be any change in something that was succeeding?

His life began to fall apart. His home disintegrated. He was lonely and miserable. His wealth and success ceased to be satisfying. A business associate suggested he might find help in the very church he had driven by so many times. And sure enough, one day Don found himself sitting in the congregation of that church listening to a sermon. It struck home immediately. The puzzle of life was beginning to come together. That day he gave his life to Christ, and today is an ardent follower of the Savior.

That experience completely reversed his priorities.

Don, and many more like him, have come to Christ in that same manner . . . "saved on the spot."

It frequently happens like that . . . *when revival comes.*

Chapter 3

FACING THE CHALLENGE

CHAPTER 3
Facing the Challenge
(Nehemiah 2:1-20)

If we are to face the challenge of revival, we must:

   I. REGISTER THE REQUEST (1-10)
      A. The King's Power (7)
      B. The King's Provision (8)
      C. The King's Protection (9)
  II. REVIEW THE RUINS
      A. Patiently (12)
      B. Persistently (13-15)
      C. Privately (16)
 III. REMOVE THE REPROACH (17-20)
      A. A Call (17)
      B. A Calling (18)
      C. A Cooperation (18)
      D. A Claim (19-20)

Facing The Challenge

(Nehemiah 2:1-20)

I am honestly convinced that most Christians would welcome a taste of genuine revival. Before we go further, I know what you are thinking: *If this observation is true, why are so few experiencing the joy of revival in their lives today?* Answer—the majority of us are simply not willing to pay the price and face the challenge of revival.

Folks like that remind me of an interesting story I recently heard. It has to do with hunting monkeys. It seems that in some remote part of our globe an ingenious hunter developed a new technique which capitalizes on his victim's greed.

A coconut is secured, a hole is drilled in the side, and the inside is scraped out. Into the coconut is placed a small piece of candy. The monkey comes along, snoops around the coconut, and sticks his hand into the hole, which, incidently, is barely big enough for his arm. He feels around inside, finds the candy, and clutches it in his fist. End of search—beginning of problem! He cannot extricate his fist from the hole. Unless, of course, he lets go of the candy. But he is too greedy for that, so he just screams, hollers, jumps, and bangs the coconut against a tree. Soon the hunter, hearing all the commotion, comes along and seizes his prey.

Now, I think it would be safe for all of us to assume that, in the final analysis, the monkey would rather have lost the candy and saved his skin, but he wasn't willing to make the choice when it really counted.

Aren't we exactly like that! Many of us, when the acid test arises would rather let go of our greed and be turned loose in the freedom of revival, but too few of us are willing to pay the price and face the challenge; not now, anyhow.

The second chapter of Nehemiah reveals some essential elements in facing the challenge of revival. What divine insight we receive from the life of Nehemiah regarding godliness and dedication! His heart was burdened over the broken-down walls of Jerusalem. He could not keep silent and uninvolved when the Holy City, which the Psalmist called "beautiful for situation, the joy of the whole earth," was in reproach and ruin. Day and night— Jerusalem. When he awoke his first thoughts were of Jerusalem. And before he fell asleep, his evening prayer was for the ruined walls of Jerusalem.

We are faced today, in our Jerusalem, with the challenge of revival. God is waiting to see if we can be entrusted with an anointing of fresh oil. The intent of every word on each page of this book is to call each of us to face the challenge of revival today. It will mean repentance, perhaps restitution, but it will also mean revival. If we are going to face this challenge of revival we must, first of all:

REGISTER THE REQUEST

And it came about in the month Nisan, in the twentieth year of King Arta-xerxes, that wine was before him, and I took up the wine and gave it to the king. Now I had not been sad in his presence. So the king said to me, "Why is your face sad though you are not sick? This is nothing but sadness

of heart." Then I was very much
afraid. And I said to the king, "Let the
king live forever. Why should my face
not be sad when the city, the place of
my fathers' tombs, lies desolate and
its gates have been consumed by
fire?" Then the king said to me, "What
would you request?" So I prayed to
the God of heaven. And I said to the
king, "If it please the king, and if your
servant has found favor before you,
send me to Judah, to the city of my
fathers' tombs, that I may rebuild it."
Then the king said to me, the queen
sitting beside him, "How long will
your journey be, and when will you
return?" So it pleased the king to send
me, and I gave him a definite time.
And I said to the king, "If it please the
king, let letters be given me for the
governors of the provinces beyond
the River, that they may allow me to
pass through until I come to Judah,
and a letter to Asaph the keeper of the
king's forest, that he may give me
timber to make beams for the gates of
the fortress which is be the temple, for
the wall of the city, and for the house
to which I will go." And the king
granted them to me because the good

hand of my God was on me. Then I came to the governors of the provinces beyond the River and gave them the king's letters. Now the king had sent with me officers of the army and horsemen. And when Sanballat the Horonite and Tobiah the Ammonite official heard about it, it was very displeasing to them that someone had come to seek the welfare of the sons of Israel (2:1-10).

Nehemiah's request to be sent to Jerusalem was born out of a burden. His burden was not new. He had carried it in his heart for four months since his kinsmen returned with their report. For four months he mourned. For four months he fasted. And for four months he prayed before the God of heaven. His request to be the agent of revival was born out of a burden.

Nehemiah's burden was so heavy that he kept on praying, and one day God opened the door. He feared having to speak to the king, but God worked it out to the extent the king asked him, "Why is your face sad, though you are not sick? There is nothing but sadness of heart."

The moment Nehemiah's burden was almost intolerable, God answered him. And God took the initiative!

It is only the man with the heavy burden that God can trust with His work. If we do not have hearts that are burdened with conviction, we will never be fruitful in the service of the Lord. God help the church which is pastored by a man who does not feel a burden for his people. God help the children, or the young people, or the adults who have Sunday School teachers who have not felt a burden for their class. God help the children of a father who has not felt the burden for his family's spiritual condition. Revival is born out of a burden!

Note the request which Nehemiah registered. "Then the king said to me, 'What would you request?' So I prayed to the God of heaven"(2:4). Between the king's question and Nehemiah's request was prayer. This brief petition was not superficial. It was backed up by four months of intense communion with God. Many of our problems could be solved if we learned this lesson—we should not only think before we speak, but we should penetrate heaven with prayer. Many a cause has been crippled and many a revival has been ruined because someone spoke before they prayed!

Nehemiah's request was, "If it please the king and if your servant has found favor before you, send me to Judah, to the city of my fathers' tombs, that I may rebuild it"(2:5). He said, "Send me!" Have you ever made that request of your King? There is some job to be done. There is some victory to be won! Send me, Lord, send me!

Nehemiah's request was followed by the king's reply. The king not only complied with the request, but sent Nehemiah on his way with some important things. Nehemiah was given the king's *power*. "And I said to the king, 'If it please the king, let letters be given me for the governors of the provinces beyond the River, that they may allow me to pass through until I come to Judah' " (2:7). The king gave him letters with the royal signet attached! Nehemiah went with all the authority and power of the king! Not only was he given the king's power—he was given the king's *provision*. "And a letter to Asaph the keeper of the king's forest, that he may give me timber to make beams for the gates of the fortress which is by the temple, for the wall of the city, and for the house to which I will go. And the king granted them to me because

the good hand of my God was on me"
(2:8).

The king gave him timber and materials
for rebuilding of those broken walls. And
that is not all—he was also given the king's
protection. "Then I came to the governors
of the provinces beyond the River and
gave them the king's letters. Now the king
had sent with me officers of the army and
horsemen"(2:9). The king sent a patrol
along to protect Nehemiah!

Let me ask you, have you lately sought
your King who has all this for you? Are you
living out of His power and authority?
Jesus said, "As the Father hath sent me,
even so send I you." Are you living out of
His provision? The Bible promises us that
God will "supply all your needs according
to his riches in glory by Christ Jesus." Are
you living out of His protection? Jesus said
he is in the Father and he is in us and we
are in him. That's pretty good company.
Nothing can harm us which he does not
allow.

Are you a child of the King? Then, are
you living with the King's power, provision, and protection? If not, why not? If we
are to face the challenge of revival, we
must begin by registering the request to be
the agent of revival. "Lord, send me!" Use

me as your agent in revival. And if we will register this request, God will be faithful to give us his power, his provision, and his protection.

In facing this challenge of revival we must not only register the request but, secondly, we must:

REVIEW THE RUINS

So I came to Jerusalem and was there three days. And I arose in the night, I and a few men with me. I did not tell any one what my God was putting into my mind to do for Jerusalem and there was no animal with me except the animal on which I was riding. So I went out at night by the Valley Gate in the direction of the Dragon's Well and on to the Refuse Gate, inspecting the walls of Jerusalem which were broken down and its gates which were consumed by fire. Then I passed on to the Fountain Gate and the King's Pool, but there was no place for my mount to pass. So I went up at night by the ravine and inspected the wall. Then I entered the Valley Gate again and returned. And the officials

did not know where I had gone or
what I had done; nor had I as yet
told the Jews, the priests, the nobles,
the officials, or the rest who did the
work (2:11-16).

Upon his arrival in Jerusalem, Nehemiah
spent three days there without ever inspecting the walls. I have often wondered
what he was doing. I think I know—I
believe he was spending time with God
counting the cost!

As we will see in coming chapters there
were all sorts of opposition to his
building—lies were spread, there was
ridicule, harassment, conspiracies against
him. But he was God's man and had a
word from God.

So after these three days of counting the
cost, he arose in the middle of the night,
mounted a donkey, went out into the
shadows through the Valley Gate, and inspected the broken down walls around
Jerusalem. In some places the ruin was so
massive that he had to dismount and
stumble over the wreckage himself. In the
middle of the night, while others were
sleeping, Nehemiah with a burdened and
desperate heart reviewed the ruins.

Can you imagine his grief that moonlit

night as he saw the devastation of his beloved Jerusalem? Whenever a real work of God is about to be done, some faithful, burdened servant has to take a journey such as Nehemiah's—to weep in the night over the ruins, to wrestle in some dark Gethsemane in prayer.

Notice especially how Nehemiah reviewed the ruins. He reviewed them cautiously and *patiently.* "And I arose in the night, I and a few men with me. I did not tell any one what my God was putting into my mind to do for Jerusalem and there was no animal with me except the animal on which I was riding" (2:12). He was led by the Spirit!

He reviewed them conscientiously. "So I went out that night by the Valley Gate in the direction of the Dragon's Well and on to the Refuse Gate, inspecting the walls of Jerusalem which were broken down and its gates which were consumed by fire. Then I passed on to the Fountain Gate and the King's Pool, but there was no place for my mount to pass. So I went up at night by the ravine and inspected the wall. Then I entered the Valley Gate again and returned" (2:13-15).

He reviewed the ruins *persistently.* He saw things as they were! It is essential that we do that in our own lives—face the facts, review the ruins. We could go on talking about how great we are. But too much of our evaluation is based on the world's strandards. How do we face up to God's standards?

How long has it been since you have ridden around your walls and seen the need for repair? Strained relationships, lovelessness, robbing God, lack of family worship, too little fruit, ad nauseum! Nehemiah not only reviewed the ruins cautiously and conscientiously, but he reviewed them independently, "And the officials did not know where I had gone or what I had done; nor had I as yet told the Jews, the priests, the nobles, the officials, or the rest who did the work" (2:16). He reviewed the ruins *privately*. The true agent of revival will not desire to be the center of attention. Nehemiah was not interested in everyone seeing what a burden he had. He was only interested in revival, the rebuilding of those broken walls.

We will never face the challenge of revival until we review the ruins of our own lives. Are we willing to do that? Are we willing to saddle up and survey our walls? Review those ruins—do our lives honor Jesus? Do our business life, our home life, our social life, our church life honor Jesus?

In facing this urgent challenge of revival we must not only register the request, review the ruins, but finally we must:

REMOVE THE REPROACH

Then I said to them, "You see the bad situation we are in, that Jerusalem is desolate and its gates burned by fire. Come, let us rebuild the wall of Jerusalem that we may no longer be a reproach." And I told them how the hand of my God had been favorable to me, and also about the king's words which he had spoken to me. Then they said, "Let us arise and build." So they put their hands to the good work. But when Sanballat the Horonite, and Tobiah, the Ammonite official, and Geshem the Arab heard it, they mocked us and despised us and said, "What is this thing you are doing? Are you rebelling against the king?" So I answered them and said to them, "The God of heaven will give us success; therefore we His servants will arise and build, but you have no portion, right, or memorial in Jerusalem." (2:17-20)

In facing the challenge of revival, how is the reproach of our broken-down walls removed? As we see in the above text, removing the reproach involves, first of all, a *call.* "Then I said to them. 'You see the bad situation we are in, that Jerusalem is desolate and its gates burned by fire. Come, let us rebuild the wall of Jerusalem that we may no longer be a reproach' " (2:17). Nehemiah reviewed the situation, and then called his cohorts to the task of rebuilding the wall. Why? "That we may no longer be a reproach!" The rebuilt walls would end the exposed condition of the city which constantly invited attacks and reproaches from the enemy. God is issuing the same call to us today. He is calling us to rebuild broken-down spiritual walls. Why? Because we must no longer be a reproach to God!

Removing the reproach also involved a *calling.* "And I told them how the hand of my God had been favorable to me, and also about the king's words which he had spoken to me. Then they said. 'Let us arise and build.' So they put their hands to the good work." (2:18). The hand of God was upon him! Nehemiah had the hand of God upon him! He had a calling to be the rebuilder of the broken walls. Friends, when we are born again, we have a special calling from God. There are no eithers, ors, ifs, or buts! The hand of God is upon us, and we must acknowledge his calling. We are commissioned to be the agents of revival. We are commanded to be filled with the Holy Spirit. We are commanded to be soulwinners for Jesus.

Removing the reproach also involves a *cooperation*. "And I told them how the hand of my God had been favorable to me, and also about the king's words which he had spoken to me. Then they said, 'Let us arise and build.' So they put their hands to the good work" (2:18). "Let us arise and build!" Unity and cooperation were to be the keys in the rebuilding of the broken walls, as we will see in coming chapters. All along the wall the people worked. There was no separation. There were no divisive spirits. There was one vision and one purpose! No church where people are at odds with each other has ever seen revival. Most churches wrestle on their knees against their real enemy, Satan. The church of the Lord Jesus ought to be engaged in one supreme task, that of reaching this world for Jesus. We need fresh oil—a fresh anointing. And if we are to ever remove the reproach we must move together in unity, each esteeming the other better than himself. It takes only a few negative spirits to throw water on the fires of revival. And what a dangerous thing to do before a holy God.

And finally we see that removing the reproach also involves a *claim*. "But when Sanballat the Horonite, and Tobiah the Ammonite official, and Geshem the Arab heard it, they mocked us and despised us and said, 'What is this thing you are doing? Are you rebelling against the king?' So I answered them and said to them, 'The God of heaven will give us success; therefore we His servants will arise and build, but you have no portion, right, or memorial in Jerusalem.' "(2:19-20)

God will give us success! Claim that promise and believe it—by faith! When God is about to sweep through in revival we can expect opposition. Satan will make a desperate attempt to divert our attention, as seen in verse 19. "But when Sanballat the Horonite, and Tobiah the Ammonite official, and Geshem the Arab heard it, they mocked us and despised us and said, 'What is this thing you are doing? Are you rebelling against the king?' " As soon as Nehemiah said, "Let us arise and build," the enemy said, "Let us arise and stop him!" It is the same today. There is no serious opposition until a Christian gets serious about claiming the promises of God. Satan is not concerned about a Christian until he sees him crowning Jesus as Lord and seeking to glorify Jesus through his life. I wonder—does our service for Jesus cause Satan to worry at all?

There is good news in the final verse! "So I answered them and said to them, 'The God of heaven will give us success; therefore we His servants will arise and build, but you have no portion, right, or memorial in Jerusalem' " (2:20). The victory is the Lord's! And the devil has no place or portion! Would you claim that promise with me today? God is willing, wanting, and longing to send a great revival to our land. Believe it!

I really wonder. Are we ready to face the challenge of revival? If so, we must *register the request.* "Send me, Lord, send me." Next, we must *review the ruins.* We can never face the challenge of revival until we are willing to saddle up and survey our own broken walls. And finally, in facing the challenge of revival we must *remove the reproach.* "Come, let us rebuild the wall of Jerusalem that we may no longer be a reproach" (2:17).

Nehemiah abandoned his pride to be the agent of revival. Are we willing to do that today? Are we willing to be abandoned to the will of God? Are we willing to be as a seed dropped into the earth—abandoned—or would we rather be a seed all shined up in a showcase so people can come by and talk about how talented and how spiritual we are. But there we are alone and dead!

Do you know what happens to a seed that is willing to be abandoned and dropped into the earth? It swells and breaks. It breaks! It loses its identity. The roots go down—and the shoots go up! Do you know what happens to all the starch in that little seed? It turns into sugar! And then that little seed begins to produce other seed just like itself! Oh, that's what we need today! That's when revival comes! That's the way we face the challenge of revival!

Have you faced the challenge of revival? Are you a seed on exhibit, or in the ground?

AN ENCOUNTER CLOSER THAN THE THIRD KIND

It was Sunday evening, and this newly married couple was out for a Sunday drive. They happened by the parking lot of the First Baptist Church. For some reason unknown to both of them, they found themselves driving into that parking lot. She asked, "What are we doing here?" He replied, "I don't know, but I just feel like we're supposed to go in the church tonight."

Once inside they heard the gospel and both were saved. Dick and Doris became members of the First Baptist Church, Fort Lauderdale. They became a part of the aggressive evangelism program of the church and today share their witness without hesitation.

It was Dick and Doris who loved into the

Kingdom the mysterious, unshaven old man who sat beside them. They had become Christians only a few weeks before.

They have since moved to another city and have joined a church there, and they continue to serve the Lord.

Occurrences like this will not be uncommon . . . when revival comes.

Chapter 4

WHEN GOD DOES A WORK

CHAPTER 4
When God Does A Work

(Nehemiah 4:1-23)

When God does a work, we must:

I. EXPECT OPPOSITION! (1-10)
   A. From Without (2,3,7)
   B. From Within (10)
II. ELIMINATE OBSTACLES! (10-13)
   A. An Impossible Platform (10)
      "building on rubbish"
   B. An Improper Perspective (12)
      "lived too close to enemy"
III. EMPHASIZE THE OFFENSIVE! (14-23)
   A. A Truth to Apply (14f) "don't leave
      the building for the battle"
   B. A Triumph to Anticipate (18,20)
      "rallying point"

When God Does A Work

(Nehemiah 4:1-23)

When God does a work—when revival really comes—it is party time! Crank up the ice-cream freezer, clean off the patio furniture, invite the friends. It is time to celebrate. Revival has come! No more problems! No more letdowns! No more obstacles!

Sounds great, doesn't it? Unfortunately, nothing could be further from the truth. When God does a work of genuine revival, sin is exposed. And this makes the devil and his crowd fighting mad! Like ham and eggs, steak and potatoes, corned beef and cabbage, revival and opposition go hand-in-hand!

The Word of God is careful to advise us what we can expect when God does a

work. First, when God does a work, we
must:

EXPECT OPPOSITION!

*Now it came about that when San-
ballat heard that we were rebuilding
the wall, he became furious and
very angry and mocked the Jews.
And he spoke in the presence of his
brothers and the wealthy men of
Samaria and said, "What are these
feeble Jews doing? Are they going
to restore it for themselves? Can they
offer sacrifices? Can they finish in a
day? Can they revive the stones
from the dusty rubble even the
burned ones?" Now Tobiah the
Ammonite was near him and he
said, "Even what they are
building—if a fox should jump on it,
he would break their stone wall
down!" Hear, O our God, how we
are despised! Return their reproach
on their own heads and give them
up for plunder in a land of captivity.
Do not forgive their iniquity and let
not their sin be blotted out before
Thee, for they have demoralized the
builders. So we built the wall and
the wall was joined together to half*

its height, for the people had a mind to work. Now it came about when Sanballat, Tobiah, the Arabs, the Ammonites, and the Ashdodites heard that the repair of the walls of Jerusalem went on, and the breaches began to be closed, they were very angry. And all of them conspired together to come and fight against Jerusalem and to cause a disturbance in it. But we prayed to our God, and because of them we set up a guard against them day and night. Thus in Judah it was said, "The strength of the burden bearers is failing, Yet there is much rubbish; And we ourselves are unable to rebuild the wall." (4:1-10).

As we see in these above verses, when God really does a work we can expect opposition. First of all, Nehemiah's opposition came from *without*. When the rebuilding of the broken walls got under way, Sanballat, Tobiah, and the others were quick to rear their heads in opposition.

I often wonder about the work for God that never causes the devil to rise up and oppose. I used to be very bothered by un-

Christlike opposition until I discovered what it was! With every passing day and every fresh insight, I become more convinced: when God does a work we can expect opposition to occur.

This opposition from without will take the form of ridicule. Tobiah yelled, "Even what they are building—if a fox should jump on it, it would break their stone wall down" (4:3). When God is doing a work, the enemy will lie to you and try to get you to believe your task is impossible. When God does a work in our lives we can look for ridicule to come. There is the ridicule of a father and mother heaped upon the young person who has a desire to grow like Jesus. There is the ridicule of a boyfriend piled on his girl when she suggests they center their lives around the Lord Jesus. There is the ridicule of the self-righteous who listens to the message of being filled with the Spirit and of holiness and snorts, "That is fanatical. That is extreme. I got Jesus when I was saved, and that is all that matters."

This opposition from without also manifested itself in an amazing fashion. "Now it came about when Sanballat, Tobiah, the Arabs, the Ammonites, and the Ashdodites heard that the repair of the walls of Jerusalem went on, and that the breaches began to be closed, they were very angry. And all of them conspired together to come and fight against Jerusalem and to cause a disturbance in it'' (4:7-8).

How amazing that these warring factors had suddenly buried their differences and had come together to oppose Nehemiah! Jesus suffered all this ridicule and the powerful force of the enemy. Do you remember what happened near the end of his life? "Now Herod and Pilate became friends with one another that very day; for before they had been at enmity with each other" (Luke 23:12). Jesus' holy life and the revival he brought caused his enemies to bury their differences and join forces against him. When God does a work we should not expect any less. Opposition from without—it is to be expected!

Perhaps you are saying, "I don't know what you are talking about! I have no opposition from without. I've not offended anyone. I don't know what you mean by ridicule." Before you are too quick to congratulate yourself it may be that Satan doesn't think you are worth bothering with!

This opposition from without resulted in

anger. Verse one says that the enemy was "very angry." What were they angry about? There was no logical reason to keep Nehemiah from rebuilding those walls. Sanballat really had no sound argument against the rebuilding of the walls, and this is what made him angry! The only reason for the anger of the enemy was the demonstration of the power of God. It is always so.

Satan has one focal point of attack here on earth—the Holy Spirit. And whenever he sees a work of the Holy Spirit, Satan concentrates his forces upon it. The very fact that a work is of God will always arouse the opposition of the enemy. The same is true today! The lost world is always opposed to the gospel. In fact, the world will always be angry at any message which exposes sin!

When God does a work we can expect opposition. This opposition will be from without, but also from *within!* Look at verse 10! "Thus in Judah it was said, 'The strength of the burden bearer is failing, Yet there is much rubbish; And we ourselves are unable to rebuild the wall.' " Here is internal trouble. Judah of all people! Here is the cream of the army filled with discouragement and threatening to revolt. "We are getting weak and feeble . . . too much rubbish . . . to big a job!''

After opposition from without and opposition from within, how easy it would have been for Nehemiah to leave for Persia, acquire his former position as the cupbearer to the king, and live a normal life. But Nehemiah never contemplated it! You see, when God really is about to move and do a work, we can expect warfare. In fact, we must expect opposition.

What did Nehemiah do about this opposition? ''So we built the wall and the whole wall was joined together to half its height, for the people had a mind to work. But we prayed to our God, and because of them we set up a guard against day and night'' (4:6,9). How was all this opposition overcome? Did Nehemiah panic, worry, retaliate? ''So we built the wall . . . ''

''The people had a mind to work!'' They had a heart to pray! They knew that prayer was the battleground in the victorious life! Many of us are running around trying to win the war of the victorious life, and some of us have never even discovered where the battlefield is. Of course, it is in the place of prayer. But not only did they have a mind to work and a heart to pray, they had an eye to watch! They kept on the alert to the forces of the enemy. We allow our enemy to creep in all too often without ever recognizing him! Friend, when God does a work, be on the alert—and expect opposition!

As we continue in our text we see that when God does a work we not only must expect opposition but we must also:

ELIMINATE OBSTACLES!

Thus in Judah it was said, "The strength of the burden bearers is failing, yet there is much rubbish; And we ourselves are unable to rebuild the wall." And our enemies said, "They will not know or see until we come among them, kill them, and put a stop to the work." And it came about when the Jews who lived near them came and told us ten times, "They will come up against us from every place where you may turn," then I stationed men in the lowest parts of the space behind the wall, the exposed places, and I stationed the people in families with their swords, spears, and bows (4:10-13).

How true it was that the walls were in shambles. On Nehemiah's night journey he had to dismount because the rubbish was so dense. When God does a work we must be careful to eliminate the obstacles.

An Impossible Platform

It is a dangerous thing to try and build a wall on a foundation as shabby as rubbish. The rubbish had to be removed!

Many people are trying to do that today—build on rubbish. They are trying to find a way to rebuild their broken relationship with Jesus without disturbing the rubbish. "Oh, I want to be Spirit-filled, I want to be pleasing to Jesus, but I will not remove the rubbish. I still want to go to those same movies. I still want to attend the same night spots. I still want to misuse my body in the same ways. I still want to be popular, so I still have to run around with certain people of the devil's crowd." I confess to you that almost every day a fresh heap of rubbish is discovered in my life which I hardly knew existed.

All our rubbish—pride, doubt, anger, evil desires, misguiding ambitions—leads to dry, barren lives for God. What a foul heap it is and how much the Temple of the Holy Spirit has been retarded because of it.

To risk putting those walls up on that kind of rubbish would simply have meant that even before they were completed, they would have fallen down again. It was essential to Nehemiah's task that the foundation should be cleared away and the work should be built upon the rock.

What about the walls you are building? Are you building them upon rubbish? If so, this message is a call for you to eliminate the obstacles, to remove the rubbish. The Bible says, "If we confess our sins, he is faithful and righteous to forgive us our sins and to cleanse us from all unrighteousness" (1 John 1:9). The work of excavating (confession and repentance) must come first. The rubbish must go!

Do you see what is happening? This is the reason so many people rebuild their walls only to see them crumble after a few days and weeks. Then they let them lie there awhile and then try to rebuild on them again. A few more weeks pass, and then they crumble again! Could it be that many of us are building on rubbish? We need to clean away the rubbish in our lives and build upon on solid rock.

An Improper Perspective

Part of our problem today is seen in verse 12. "And it came about when the Jews who lived near them came and told us ten times, 'They will come up against us from every place where you may turn,' " (4:12). Some of the Jews were living too close to the enemy. They weren't living near the center of the glow of the spiritual force and power of God. All they were conscious of was the opposition. I wonder how many today are living dangerously close to the enemy. No close contact with God's work. No wonder we are so afraid to step out on faith. All we have been listening to is the devil's lies, his deceit, and his doubts!

The Lord Jesus is ready at the door of our hearts to fill the garbage truck of all our rubbish—and take it away. Then and only then is when we ought to begin to rebuild those broken walls.

We have seen that when God does a work we must expect opposition, we must eliminate obstacles, but finally we also must:

EMPHASIZE THE OFFENSIVE!

When I saw their fear, I rose and
spoke to the nobles, the officials,
and the rest of the people: "Do not
be afraid of them; remember the
Lord who is great and awesome,
and fight for your brothers, your
sons, your daughters, your wives,
and your houses." And it happened
when our enemies heard that it was
known to us, and that God had
frustrated their plan, then all of us
returned to the wall, each one to his
work. And it came about from that
day on, that half of my servants carried on the work while half of them
held the spears, the shields, the
bows, and the breastplates; and the
captains who were rebuilding the
wall and those who carried burdens
took their load with one hand doing
the work and the other holding a
weapon. As for the builders, each
wore his sword girded at his side as
he built, while the trumpeter stood
near me. And I said to the nobles,
the officials, and the rest of the people, "The work is great and extensive, and we are separated on the

wall far from one another. At whatever place you hear the sound of the
trumpet, rally to us there. Our God
will fight for us." So we carried on
the work with half of them holding
spears from dawn until the stars appeared. At that time I also said to the
people, "Let each man with his servant spend the night within
Jerusalem so that they may be a
guard for us by night and a laborer
by day" (4:14-23).

A Truth to Apply

One of the pivotal truths of this chapter is
that the people of God are not to stop the
building to do battle. To battle always is to
play defense. But we are on the offensive
and God will fight for us. We must emphasize the offensive "when God does a
work." It would have been easy for
Nehemiah to answer scorn with scorn and
leave the walls to fight the enemy. That is
exactly what the devil would love to see all
of us do.

At this point we see a mighty principle.
Half of the people were at work, and half of
the people were at watch. They worked
with weapons in one hand and a tool in the

other. You see, we must be armed for our warfare. But the battling must never replace the building of the Temple of God. The defensive must never replace the offensive. We must emphasize the offensive. The wall must go up to the glory of God. Nehemiah got on with the job, even as he battled with the foe. His principle was never to leave the building for the battle.

What a tremendous lesson! Too many people today have left the building for the battle. Someone has said something against us. Someone has wronged us. And we have allowed Satan to divert our attention. We have gotten on the defensive. We have forgotten about the building, and now it is crumbling. And all we can think about is the battle.

This is the obvious tactic and trick of the devil. He wants to divert us from Jesus, put our eyes on the problem instead of the problem solver. He wants to get us involved in the battle instead of the building. He wants us to play defense instead of offense. Oh, learn a lesson from Nehemiah. Never leave the building for the battle, Empasize the offensive.

A Triumph to Anticipate

One of the most thrilling parts of this whole passage is in verse 20. "At whatever place you hear the sound of the trumpet, rally to us there. Our God will fight for us." Nehemiah had a rallying point for his whole army. Verse 18 tells us he kept the trumpeter always by his side. The workers were widely scattered all along the wall and laboring at the same time. At the sound of the trumpet they all were to leave their work and rally around Nehemiah for the final overthrow of the enemy. The focal point of all their strategy was their commander and the trumpet was the signal to gather. They expected to win—and they did.

Need I say any more? All across the world today missionaries, preachers, lay people, and others are scattered, working on the building of God! Some of the ranks are thin, some are cut off from fellowship, but they are building. We all have one premier commander, the Lord Jesus Christ. He is the rallying point for all of us. And one day the trumpet shall sound, we shall leave our work, put down our tools, and rally around Him. One day soon after that the enemy will be completely over-thrown.

How thrilling it is to know that we are in the fight. One day the work will be over, the trumpet will sound, and Jesus will come! In the words of H. L. Turner:

It may be at morn when the day is awakening,
When sunlight through darkness and shadow is breaking
That Jesus will come in the fullness of glory
To receive from the world His own.

It may be at midday, it may be at twilight.
It may be, perchance, that the black-ness of midnight
Will burst into light in the blaze of His glory
When Jesus receives His own.

Oh, Lord Jesus, how long, how long,
Ere we hear that glad song,
Christ returneth, Hallelujah,
Hallelujah, Amen!

But until then, we must go up with the

buildng of God and emphasize the offensive!

God is willing, waiting, and longing to do a reviving work in our land and lives today. When the conditions for revival are met and when revival comes, God will do a powerful work. And when God does a work, there are certain things we must expect. We must expect opposition. We must, then, eliminate the obstacles. We must remove the rubbish. And finally we must continue to emphasize the offensive. We must never leave the building for the battle.

This message is a call to all of us to remove the rubbish in our own lives! The pride, the anger, the worry, the broken relationships. All of those sins which are rubbish in our lives. We cannot build a Spirit-filled life on foundations such as those. We must lay them aside and build to the glory of God!

ATMOSPHERIC CONVICTION

He had no church affiliation. His wife was a topless dancer. Their existence held no place for God. He was driving down Broward Boulevard and came to the corner of NE Third Avenue, the corner where the First Baptist Church is located.

He glanced over at the church and fell under a strange conviction. He looked at the sign and saw the pastor's name. Arriving at home he immediately called me. "Pastor," he said, "You don't know me. My name is Bob. I need help."

He came to the office. His first words were, "Preacher, I pulled up to the stop light, and when I looked over at the church I began to see every sin I had committed in my lifetime." He then proceeded to give a history of his godless life. In a few moments he was gloriously saved. He was baptized the next Sunday. His wife was saved within a few days.

They both are serving the Lord now.

There are times when there is a clearly-defined zone of heavenly influence . . . *when revival comes.*

Chapter 5

THE ENEMY'S PLOT

CHAPTER 5

The Enemy's Plot

(Nehemiah 6:1-19)

Satan will attempt to:

I. MANIPULATE OUR MINDS (1-3)

II. MISREPRESENT OUR MOTIVES (5-7)

III. MODIFY OUR MISSION (10)

IV. MISGUIDE OUR MODELS (17-19)

The Enemy's Plot

(Nehemiah 6:1-19)

As we come to chapter six of Nehemiah we read some of the most important words in the whole book, "So the wall was completed" (6:15). It sounds the note of victory in the conquest of the enemy. But this shout of triumph did not come without a final, last-ditch attempt by the enemy to delay the rebuilding and quench the fires of revival.

There is extensive talk about revival in many circles today. And every week we see more and more people "getting in on what God is up to." It will do us well to remember, however, that the devil is violently opposed to the moving of God's Spirit in revival. Make no mistake about it, when the people of God say, "Let us arise and build," Satan raises his ugly head, wrings his wretched hands, and says, "Let us arise and stop them!"

Satan has a plot to divert us and steer us away from holiness. This chapter is designed to expose the enemy's plot and to teach us how to overcome him that it might also be said of us, "So the wall was completed." As these principles are understood and are applied in our lives, we will live in victory over the devil and continue with the work of rebuilding our spiritual walls.

The plot of the enemy is four-fold. We see, first of all, that he will attempt to:

MANIPULATE OUR MINDS

Now it came about when it was reported to Sanballat, Tobiah, to Geshem the Arab, and to the rest of our enemies that I had rebuilt the wall, and that no breach remained in it although at that time I had not set up the doors in the gates, that Sanballat and Geshem sent a message to me, saying, "Come, let us meet together at Chephirim in the plain of Ono." But they were planning to harm me. So I sent messen-

*gers to them, saying, "I am doing a
great work and I cannot come
down. Why should the work stop
while I leave it and come down to
you?" (6:1-3)*

Here we find Nehemiah hard at work on
the rebuilding of the broken walls of
Jerusalem. Sanballat and Geshem were
saying, "Come down to the plain, and we
will meet together. Come on down on our
level. Don't be so fanatical and extreme.
You are too narrow. Come on down to our
level, down to the plain, and let's reason
this thing out!"

The devil is always trying to manipulate
our minds by telling us that we need to
compromise. He is always trying to get us
to live by reason and not by faith and trust
in God. He simply wants us to compromise, to come down to the plain. After
all, everybody else is doing it! Why should
we be so extreme? Satan is chiefly concerned with manipulating our minds to the
point that he will lead us to compromise.

What was Nehemiah's reaction to this
subtle plot of the enemy? Listen to his reply: "I am doing a great work and I cannot
come down. Why should the work stop
while I leave it and come down to you?"

(6:3) How thrilling this is! There was no compromise with Nehemiah. After all, why should he cease God's work to get down on the level with the agents of Satan?

Now, a more pointed question—What will you do? The devil is out to manipulate your mind. He is out to get you to compromise, to drag you down to the plains, down to his level!

I can predict what you will do. You will follow one of two courses. (1) You will compromise. You will go down to the plain! Someone will come along, a tool of the devil, and say, "Come on down to the plain with me. Let down your spiritual and moral guard, and come on down to the plain, down on my level. Cut the corner with me on that business deal. Live in sin with me on Friday night. No one will know. Come on down to the plain." And you will leave the rebuilding of your spiritual walls, compromise with the devil, and go down to the plain. *or,* (2) You will say, "I am doing a great work for God, and I cannot come down." When the devil raises his ugly head, when he tempts you to come down to the plain, why don't you say that? Friend, open your eyes to his subtle tactics and his devilish plot. He is out to manipulate our minds!

As we go further into the text, we see that if he fails here to manipulate our minds he will try to:

MISREPRESENT OUR MOTIVES

Then Sanballat sent his servant to me in the same manner a fifth time with an open letter in his hand. In it was written, "It is reported among the nations, and Gashmu says, that you and the Jews are planning to rebel; therefore you are rebuilding the wall. And you are to be their king, according to these reports. "And you have also appointed prophets to proclaim in Jerusalem concerning you, 'A king is in Judah!' And now it will be reported to the king according to these reports. So come now, let us take counsel together" (6:57).

If the devil cannot get us to compromise, he will spread rumors about us and try to misrepresent our motives! Just watch! If a Christian is all out for souls and has a heart for God, he most likely will become the target for other people's tongues. The devil will see to that! Few people give a man of God credit for speaking only to the glory of God. If we really become sold out to Jesus and filled with the Spirit of God, we shouldn't be surprised when the devil fabricates lies about us. He will misrepresent our motives!

What was Nehemiah's reaction to this second plot to halt revival? Listen to his reply, "Such things as you are saying have not been done, but you are inventing them in your own mind. You are trying to frighten us and discourage us so that the work will not be done . . . But now, O God, strengthen my hands" (6:8-9).

Those lies did not divert Nehemiah one inch! Satan's attempt to get him all hot and bothered by misrepresenting his motives failed miserably! How thrilling this is. Nehemiah was not concerned in what others thought about him. He had one consuming passion in life—to rebuild those broken walls, What a lesson for us!

Now, again, the more pointed question: What will you do? Friend, the devil is out to misrepresent your motives. Satan will try the same tactic on you that he did on Nehemiah—that is, if you are dedicated to revival. You may be saying, "I do not quite understand all this. Satan has never tried to misrepresent my motives. I am not really bothered by Satan.'' Before you are too quick to congratulate yourself, you ought to search your life and see if there is anything in it that would even cause Satan to be bothered!

When Satan misrepresents our motives, when some agent of the devil says we are seeking our own glory, I dare you to stand with Nehemiah and answer, ''Such things as you are saying have not been true, for you are inventing them in your own mind.''

Open your eyes to the devil's subtle points. He will try to manipulate our minds, he will try to misrepresent our motives, and if both of these attempts fail, he will then try to:

MODIFY OUR MISSION

And when I entered the house of Shemaiah the son of Delaiah, son of Mehetabel, who was confined at home, he said. ''Let us meet together in the house of God, within the temple, and let us close the doors of the temple, for they are coming to kill you, and they are coming to kill you at night'' (6:10).

Here in verse 10, this man, posing as a prophet, urged Nehemiah to flee to the Temple and stay there, lest the enemy should slay him. He tried to persuade Nehemiah into an easy-going, compromising religion. This was Satan's third plot, to modify Nehemiah's mission. He wanted him to forget the wall for a while and retreat to the Temple. Now, there was nothing wrong with the Temple. It was a good place to be. It just wasn't out there on the cutting edge, and it simply was not where God had put Nehemiah!

Satan here was attempting to induce Nehemiah into shirking his responsibilities. He was attempting to attract him with a cheap religion that would not compel him to carry a cross!

This is one of the enemy's plots. The devil is out to modify our mission. He tries to involve us in "good" things, but things without the power of the Holy Spirit and the message of salvation. If you do not believe it, merely look around at other churches today. The devil has modified their mission. They once reached out with the message of salvation, and today they have modified their mission and are struggling to make their budgets and watching their memberships decline with every passing year.

Oh, they are doing good things! They are interested in feeding the hungry and clothing the naked. They see the prodigal son out in the pig pen. They are quick to put food in his belly, clothes on his back, a few dollars in his pocket, but they leave him in the pigpen! The mission of the church is to direct that boy back to the Father's house. There the Father feeds him, puts a robe on his back, shoes on his feet, a ring on his finger, and supplies all his needs according to His own riches. Friend, Satan is out to modify our mission.

What was Nehemiah's reaction to this third plot to halt revival? Listen to his reply: "Should a man like me flee? And could one such as I go into the temple to save his life? I will not go in!" (6:11). Nehemiah was committed to his mission, the rebuilding of those broken walls! And nothing, not even the devil, could modify that mission.

Again, a more pointed question—What will *you* do? Satan will come to you and seek to modify your mission if he hasn't already. He doesn't want you to be a soul-winner. He doesn't want you to be a Bible student. He doesn't want you to be filled with the Spirit. He doesn't want you to deny yourself. He doesn't want you to take up your cross daily. He doesn't want you to follow Jesus. And he will seek to divert you by modifying your mission. He will get you interested, if he can, in "good" things but not the right things!

I call on you to learn a lesson from Nehemiah. Don't take the easy way. There is a job to be done in the rebuilding of spiritual walls in your life. Take up your cross and follow Jesus.

The enemy has a final plot to divert us from revival. If he fails in manipulating our minds, misrepresenting our motives, modifying our mission, then he will attempt to:

MISGUIDE OUR MODELS

Also in those days many letters went from the nobles of Judah to Tobiah, and Tobiah's letters came to them. For many in Judah were bound by oath to him because he was the son-in-law of Shecaniah the son of Arah, and his son Jehohanan had married the daughter of Meshullam the son of Berechiah. Morever, they were speaking about his good deeds in my presence and reported my words to him. Then Tobiah sent letters to frighten me (6:17-19).

Here we see an amazing situation! Judah is corresponding with the enemy and telling them every move that Nehemiah is making! Judah, of all people! Judah—in the lineage of Jesus! Judah, this model tribe, had been misguided by the enemy.

Satan surely reasoned that when Judah turned its back on the work of God, Nehemiah would say, "What's the use?" and throw in the towel.

Do you see this subtle plot, the misguiding of our models, being exposed before us? Satan will try to divert real revival by misguiding our models. It is dangerous to have a model of anyone in the Christian life apart from the Lord Jesus. Often we hear someone say, "Oh, if I could just be the Christian that Mary is." Or "If I just had the faith of Bill." Listen, friend, if you start putting your eyes on someone else as a model in the Christian faith, the devil will seek to misguide your models! Remember, if Satan cannot defeat you, he will defeat a model whose defeat will defeat you!

Here is a warning—keep your eyes on Jesus and no one else. If you have a model in the Christian life apart from the Lord Jesus, Satan is out to misguide that model in order to divert you from real revival.

Friend, just because the devil has a plot does not mean we need to fall victim to it. Even though he attempted to manipulate Nehemiah's mind, misrepresent his motives, modify his mission, and misguide his models, we recognize that he failed miserably and, "the wall was finished." Praise the Lord!

The same can apply to our lives today! We can live in victory over the devil.

Nehemiah is but a foreshadow of Jesus. Look at the Lord Jesus. Satan tried these same plots on him. He tried to *manipulate his mind*. He told Nehemiah to "come on down to the plain." Listen to what he told the Lord Jesus through the scoffers around the cross. "If you are really God, come on down from the cross." Can you hear Jesus' reply? I am sure it was closely akin to Nehemiah's, "I cannot come down, I'm doing God's work!"

Satan also tried to *misrepresent his motives*. The devil's crowd accused Jesus of being a friend to sinners and a winebibber. They ridiculed him for healing on the sabbath, and a hundred other things. Every time he did something to the glory of God, there was someone there to misrepresent his motive. They accused Nehemiah of trying to be a king. They called Jesus "the King of the Jews."

The devil also tried to *modify his mission*. The devil tried to steer Nehemiah away from the walls and go to the Temple. He did the same with the Lord Jesus. He wanted Jesus to take the easy, expedient way. He would have liked for Jesus to call down twelve legions of angels to remove him from the cross and set him free. With every ounce of devilish determination within him, he tempted Jesus to modify his mission.

And then, finally, when all else failed, the devil tried to *misguide his models*. The training of those twelve disciples was a difficult and enduring work of Christ during his three-year ministry. They were the models, so to speak, of the Christian faith. And the night Jesus needed them the most, the night he was arrested and tried falsely, they all forsook him and fled into the darkness. Satan wanted Jesus to give up, and ask, "what's the use?" Remember, if he cannot defeat us, he will defeat someone whose defeat will defeat us.

But Jesus was the victor over Satan and because he was, we can be also. We can live in victory over the devil. The Bible says, "Submit therefore to God. Resist the devil and he will flee from you" (James 4:7). We must submit ourselves to the Lord, confess our sins, crown Jesus Lord, and receive the fullness of the Holy Spirit. Then by the authority of the name of Jesus and by his precious blood, we can resist the devil and he wil flee from us.

Friend, if you have a heart for revival, Satan will employ these same tactics on you that he did on Nehemiah, Jesus, and millions of others. But because the devil has a plot does not mean we must fall victim to it. We can live in victory over the devil, and it can be spoken of us, "So they finished the walls."

The Holy Spirit wants to fill us, for only then can he effectively use us, and only then can we live in victory over the devil.

Have your eyes been opened? Has Satan attempted to manipulate your mind, misrepresent your motives, modify your mission, or misguide your models? I remind you, he is a defeated foe and not "alive and well on planet earth." He is alive but not well. He is terminally ill. And those of us who know Jesus and are called by His name have been given authority over the devil. Come to Jesus! Find in him your all in all!

A TYPICAL CHRISTIAN BECOMES UNTYPICAL!

She had never won a person to Jesus Christ or even faced seriously her responsibility to do so. She was simply a "typical" Christian. She was Miss Average Christian! This means that she was the best of the worst of the best.

But something happened to Robin. She fell in love anew with Jesus. She viewed life through different eyes. She saw the world through different eyes. She began to talk about her new love on her dates and soon brought her boyfriend to Christ.

Little did she know that this would begin a chain reaction. In a few weeks the boy she led to Christ led a friend of his to Christ. It was not long before the friend of the friend led his friend to Christ. It was not long before the friend of the friend of the friend of Robin brought two of his friends to Christ.

Robin had learned a vital lesson. Real evangelism is not simple addition but multiplication! As the revival gained momentum in her church, she realized that evangelism is not taught as much as it is caught.

If we will lead someone to Christ and continue to do so, and the ones won lead others to Christ and continue to do so, soon there will be a glorious end-time harvest to be presented. And I believe that this is what we can expect . . . when revival comes!

Chapter 6

AFTER REVIVAL COMES

CHAPTER 6
After Revival Comes
(Nehemiah 8)

After Revival Comes

(Nehemiah 8)

My family and I formerly lived in a beautiful little Oklahoma town, located amid the rolling hills of eastern Oklahoma. There is plenty of pride in that town. In fact, the natives referred to it as "the three-letter capital of the world." (Ada spelled backwards is Ada!)

Along one of those streets in that town, a certain church was located. I was always intrigued by a sign that dangled underneath the larger sign which identified the church. The smaller sign (which has been hanging for several years) reads, "Revival in Progress!" Friend, when revival comes we do not have to hang out a sign to advertise it. People will know it by the way we look, the way we talk, the way we act.

Until now, as we have walked together through the Book of Nehemiah, we have been dealing with circumstances and conditions which bring about revival. As we saw in the last chapter, "The walls were completed" (6:15). Revival had come. Now we are exposed to the aftermath of revival. What happens when the walls are completed? What are the circumstances in the life of the believer "after revival comes?"

There are some specific signs that always follow genuine revival. We will not need to hang out a sign to advertise them. They will be more than apparent to all those around us. If real revival has come to our hearts and lives, it will be known by several accompanying characteristics. I challenge you to examine these principles in light of your personal relationship with Christ and see if revival has come.

Let's begin by observing that after genuine revival has come to our hearts, there will be:

RECONCILIATION WITH THE SAINTS

And all the people gathered as one man at the square which was in

front of the Water Gate, and they
asked Ezra the scribe to bring the
book of the law of Moses which the
Lord had given to Israel (8:1).

Note especially these words in verse
one, "All the people gathered as one
man." There was unity in the family of
God. There was reconciliation with the
saints.

This was not so with the Israelites before
revival came. Do you remember the con-
duct of some Jews when the walls were in
the process of being rebuilt? Some were at
outs with each other. Some were pessi-
mistic and complained that the task was
too great (4:10). Later Judah betrayed
Nehemiah and reported his every word
and action to the enemy (6:17-19). There
was dissension in the camp.

But now, after the walls were completed,
after revival came, there was a unity within
the people of God. There was a beautiful
reconciliation with the saints. The Spirit of
revival brought a new love for each other,
and all the people gathered as "one man at
the square."

Friend, this is the first characteristic of
genuine revival. The people of God are in
such harmony and unity with each other
that they function as "one man." After

revival comes they are of one mind and one spirit. They hold to one hope, they have one goal, they move in one way. There is unity. There is reconciliation with the saints.

Do you remember the way Jesus said we would be known? He said, "By this shall all men know that you are my disciples . . . if you love the brethren." We can never have genuine revival without its resulting in reconciliation with one another.

Now, let me ask you a personal question—has revival come to your heart? If it has I can tell you something about yourself. You love your brothers and sisters in Christ with *agape* love. No matter what someone may do to you by insult or injury, you seek for them only their highest good. If revival has truly come to your heart, one of the apparent signs will be reconciliation with the saints.

If you are holding a grudge against someone, harboring resentment against someone, not reconciled with someone in your heart, then friend, you need revival!

This is the first sign that real revival has come—reconciliation with the saints. There is a second characteristic that always follows revival and it is:

RESPECT FOR THE SCRIPTURES

Then Ezra the priest brought the law before the assembly of men, women, and all who could listen with understanding, on the first day of the seventh month. And he read from it before the square which was in front of the Water Gate from early morning until midday, in the presence of men and women, those who could understand; and all the people were attentive to the book of the law (8:2-3).

After revival came, as the people of God gathered in one accord, Ezra the priest read from the Scriptures, and all the people were attentive. They listened with respect to the Word of God. This, too, is a watermark of genuine revival—a new love and respect for the Scriptures. Note what they did. They *read* the Word (8:3). They *revered* the Word (8:5). They *understood* the Word (7,8). And also note that they read from the Book of the Law daily (8:18).

Here is an accompanying characteristic of genuine revival. The people of God will respect the Scriptures! We cannot be in revival. We cannot stay filled with the Spirit apart from reading the Word of God daily!

Now, let me ask you a personal question—has revival come to your heart? If so, I can tell you something about yourself. You spend time every day in the Word of God. You love the Bible. It is a real part of you. You respect the Scriptures and find strength in them. Perhaps you have to admit that you do not read the Bible like you should. You do not spend time in God's Word daily. It is really not a part of your daily routine and life. Then, I write this kindly but firmly—you need revival! You need to repent of your neglect. You need to confess your sin and crown Jesus Lord of your life. A telling sign that revival has come is a respect for the Scriptures.

There is another mark of genuine revival and it is:

REVERENCE FOR THE SAVIOR

Then Ezra blessed the Lord the great God. And all the people answered, "Amen, Amen!" while lifting up their hands; then they bowed low and worshipped the Lord with their faces to the ground (8:6).

Note, thirdly, that the people began to

bless the Lord and praise him. They lifted up their hands in reverence of the Savior! They bowed low in prayer and worshipped the Lord.

Friend, after revival comes, the natural thing to do is to reverence the Savior through praise and prayer. After revival, praise and prayer are as natural as water running down a hill. We see the proof in the life of those Israelites—that we cannot have genuine revival without its resulting in praise and prayer!

The most appropriate way to approach God in prayer is through praise. The Psalmist exhorted, "Enter into His gates with thanksgiving and into His courts with praise!" God said, "Whoso offereth praise glorifieth Me!" Praise is simply adoring God for who he is. We worship God through prayer and praise! There is no possible way revival can come without its resulting in continual praise to Jesus.

May I ask you another question—has revival come to your heart? If so, I know something else about you. You not only read the Word every day, but you have a daily time of prayer and praise alone with God. You bless the Lord, praise him, bow before him, and worship him! That is a sign of genuine revival.

Perhaps, if you are honest again, you would have to examine your life and see that you have not prayed much this week. You have not worshipped and praised the Lord very much. Is that so of your life? Then, you need revival. You need to repent of your neglect, confess, crown, and claim the fullness of the Spirit of God in your life. For revival cannot come without resulting in a deeper reverence for the Savior expressed through prayer and praise.

After revival comes, there will be another identifying mark. It will always be followed by a:

RENUNCIATION OF SIN

> Then Nehemiah, who was the governor, and Ezra the priest and scribe, and the Levites who taught the people said to all the people, "This day is holy to the Lord your God; do not mourn or weep." For all the people were weeping when they heard the words of the law (8:9).

Do you grasp it? After revival comes, the

people of God stay broken over their sin. They renounce their sin. As the people heard the Word they were made conscious of their own sin and wept over it. The deeper they plunged into revival, the closer they drew to the heart of God, the more aware they became of their sin. They stayed broken over their sin.

This is always the case after revival comes. When we have really been in genuine revival, the closer we come to the heart of God, the more we realize that we are filthy rags in his sight. Every sweet taste of Calvary is accompanied by a new awareness of how unworthy and unrighteous we are. After revival comes it will always be followed by a renunciation of sin and a brokenness over our condition.

Let me ask you? Has revival come to your heart? If so, I can tell you something about yourself. You realize what you are—"filthy rags" alongside the righteousness of God. You no longer go around thinking about how important or how wonderful you are. But instead you stay broken over your sin! You weep when you think of how far short you have fallen from the Glory of God! It is a genuine sign that revival has come—a renunciation of sin.

You say, "I must be honest again! This past week my sin really hasn't bothered me that much. I haven't really been burdened about it. I have not been broken over it. Nor have I renounced my sin." Oh, dear friend, if that is the case, you need revival. You need to repent of your neglect and crown Jesus Lord of your life. For after revival comes, it is always followed by renunciation of sin. You will stay crushed over sin.

There is a final mark that always follows genuine revival. It is:

REJOICING IN SERVICE

". . . the joy of the Lord is your strength" (8:10).

After the walls were completed, after revival came, those Israelites became happy in the service of the Lord. That's always a mark—after revival comes! "The joy of the Lord was their strength." There was "great rejoicing" (8:18).

Of course, you recall when there is rejoicing in heaven—when one sinner repents. After revival comes, there is rejoicing in service and soul-winning. Do you want to know what real joy is? It is in the service of

Jesus and particularly in leading others to know him. After revival comes, we cannot help but share our faith—and rejoice in the service of Jesus.

Here is a real insight into the Word of God—the joy of the Lord is dependent upon obedience to God. If there is one characteristic of those Israelites it was obedience. Think about it—Jesus, "who for the joy that was set before Him, endured the cross, despising the shame . . ." (Heb. 12:2). Jesus found his greatest joy in doing the will of his Father!

We will never have joy, never be happy, outside the will of God for our lives. This is why so many are miserable today. This is why so many go around with a false joy on their face. Doing the will of God, obeying the commandments of God, these are the things that bring joy!

After revival comes here is another sign that it has been genuine—rejoicing in service. It is something we cannot help. When a load has been lifted, when we are obedient to the Father, when we are in His will, we cannot help but rejoice in that service.

Has revival come to your heart? If so, I know something else about you. The joy of the Lord is your strength. You are in the will of God. You are obedient to the Father.

You are a happy Christian. People see joy written all over your face. You rejoice in the service of Jesus.

You say, "I wish that were true. But if I am honest, I have to say I am not rejoicing in service. This past week I have been out of the will of God. This past week there has been no joy. This past week I have been disobedient to my heavenly Father." Friend, if this is your case, you need revival! You need to be filled with the love and joy of Jesus. For, after revival comes, it always results in rejoicing in service.

Joy is not something that is worked up, but something the Lord imparts to his children. It is his joy. It is the joy *of the Lord*. It is the fruit of the Spirit (Gal. 5:22-23). It is the outcropping of one life within. Let Jesus fill you with his Spirit, and joy will always reveal itself to other people. There is nothing as contagious as a joyful Christian.

Has genuine, Spirit-led, Spirit-filled revival come to your heart? If so, there are some marks that will be characteristic of you that always accompany true revival. There will be reconciliation with the saints. There will be respect for the Scriptures. There will be reverence for the Savior. There will be renunciation of sin. And there will be rejoicing in service. If these are not true in your life, you need revival.

And here is the way! First of all, confess every known sin up to date (I John 1:9). Next, choose against yourself (Luke 9:23). Thirdly, choose the position of death (Rom. 6:11). Next, choose the will of God over your own will (Rom. 12:1-2). Then, crown Jesus Christ Lord of your life (Rom. 14:9). And finally, praise the Lord by faith. God's command is this—"be filled with the Spirit" (Eph. 5:18). God's promise is this—"And this is the confidence which we have before Him, that, if we ask anything according to His Will, He hears us. And if we know that he hears us in whatever we ask, we know that we have the requests which we have asked from Him" (I John 5:14-15).

Go ahead—confess, and claim the fullness of God in your own life. That is when revival will come. And, after revival comes it will result in reconciliation with the saints, respect for the Scriptures, reverence for the Savior, renunciation of sin, and rejoicing in service. These are always the paramount signs . . . after revival comes!

A RUNAWAY IS CAUGHT...
BY CHRIST

She was a runaway, and all that happens to runaways seemed to happen to Lisa. You can let your imagination run loose, and all you could imagine would be evident in Lisa's broken life. She became a tool and slave of the devil and his followers. On the merry-go-round she found it impossible to let go and break with her frantic life. She could not get her wants together, and didn't know how to break free if her desires had been unanimous. She was a Pennsylvania girl and a long way from home in Florida.

At this point, two people, Bob and Carol, crossed the path of the broken girl from Pennsylvania. They understood that like the man, robbed, wounded, and left for dead on the Jericho Road, Lisa had been victimized by her world just as severely. They did not pass by on the other side. In fact, they did more than the good Samaritan. They became the innkeepers! Their home became Lisa's home. Their food became Lisa's food. And their love was heaped upon Lisa as one of their own. Because of the price that Bob and Carol paid, Lisa met Jesus. The runaway had been caught!

It was a sad-glad good-bye as Lisa boarded the plane for home, her ticket paid for by the church. But before this she had given her testimony before a packed church where she had found a spiritual home.

Runaways—what we all are by heart—generally get caught by Christ . . . when revival comes!

Chapter 7

GOING ON . . . IN REVIVAL

CHAPTER 7
Going On . . . in Revival
(Nehemiah 9)

I. CONTINUOUSLY RECEIVE OUR CLEANSING (1-3)
   Cleansing involves:
   A. The Walk of our Lives (1,2)
      "Consecration, Separation"
   B. The Work of the Law (3)
   C. The Witness of Our Lips (2,3,)
      "Confession"
   D. The Worship of the Lord (3)

II. CONSCIENTIOUSLY REVIEW OUR CALLING (5-31)
   A. Our Position- "who we are"
   B. Our Past- "where we've been"
   C. Our Potential- "where we're going"

III. CONSTANTLY RENEW OUR COMMITMENT (32-38)
   A. A Revelation   "Yesterday's victory does not suffice today."
   B. A Realization

Going On . . . In Revival

(Nehemiah 9)

Through these pages we have intensively studied about revival. We have closely examined the conditions which bring about revival. We have observed what we can expect when God does a work. We have openly revealed the obvious tactics and plots of the devil to divert us from revival. And we have examined some specific signs that always follow genuine revival.

So, we have examined revival before it comes and after it comes. Now, finally, I conclude with this important message—"Going On . . . In Revival." When revival comes the question is often asked, "Where do we go from here?" Nehemiah

9 addresses this subject very pointedly. It teaches us how to continue in a spirit of revival. It reveals some tremendous insights, which if appropriated and applied, will keep the fires of revival burning brightly days, months, even years "after revival comes."

It must be remembered that every day is a new day, and these principles outlined here are to be put into operation day by day in order to go on in revival.

If we are going on in revival we must:

CONTINUOUSLY RECEIVE
OUR CLEANSING

Now on the twenty-fourth day of this month the sons of Israel assembled with fasting, in sackcloth, and with dirt upon them. And the descendants of Israel separated themselves from all foreigners, and stood and confessed their sins and the iniquities of their fathers. While they stood in their place, they read from the book of the law of the Lord their God for a fourth of the day; and for another fourth they confessed and worshipped the Lord their God (9:1-3).

The Israelites had rebuilt the wall, Revival had come. The Feast of Tabernacles had been observed again for the first time since the days of Joshua! Nehemiah 8:17 notes, "There was great rejoicing!" Now it would have been easy for the Israelites to rest their commitment on what happened yesterday. But they had a heart to go on with God in revival. As we come to chapter 9 we see that feasting turned to fasting, and joy to humiliation. They sought and received a new, fresh touch, a cleansing from God.

The Walk Of Our Lives

The cleansing involved consecration. "Now on the twenty-fourth day of this month the sons of Israel assembled with fasting, in sackcloth, and with dirt upon them" (9:1). They humbled themselves before God. They meant business. They fasted and dressed in sackcloth. They consecrated themselves to God. As you recall, this is what brought about revival (1:4), and this is what would now keep it going.

Another step in this cleansing for the Israelites was separation. "And the descendants of Israel separated themselves from all foreigners, and stood and confessed their sins and the iniquities of their fathers'' (9:2). They sensed a need to disassociate themselves from people who were not of God. They separated themselves from all foreigners. They knew they could sink to the level of those with whom they associated. Therefore, separation was a major part in their cleansing and going on in revival.

The Word Of His Law

And then we note that they read from the Book of the Law. ''While they stood in their place, they read from the book of the law of the Lord their God for a fourth of the day; and for another fourth they confessed and worshipped the Lord their God'' (9:3). After revival came to their hearts it is interesting to note how much time they spent in the Word of God!

The Witness Of Our Lips

And then again confession played a major part. ''While they stood in their place, they read from the book of the law of the Lord their God for a fourth of the day; and for another fourth they confessed and worshipped the Lord their God" (9:3). They confessed their sin to God.

The Worship Of The Lord

And they also worshipped the Lord. "While they stood in their place, they read from the book of the law of the Lord their God for a fourth of the day; and for another fourth they confessed and worshipped the Lord their God" (9:3). They worshipped the Lord God. They didn't go through the motions, but they genuinely worshipped God.

Friend, if we are to continue in revival in our day we must begin the same way. We must continuously receive our cleansing. First of all, consecration! We must humble ourselves before God, stay desperate, and mean business with God. Then we must separate ourselves from the devil's crowd. We cannot go on in revival and run with the devil's crowd. We cannot do it!

The Bible admonishes us not to be unequally yoked together. It challenges us come out from among them and be separate (2 Cor. 6:17). We become who we run around with. So separation is a major part in going on with God. And then we note: if we are to continue in revival with a cleansing from God, we cannot do it apart from the Word of God.

And then there is confession! We must daily confess our sins to God. We must ask the Holy Spirit to reveal every sin in our lives. Then we must confess these sins individually to God. Then thank God by faith for the forgiveness and cleansing of the blood of Jesus. There is no cleansing without confession.

I often wonder how many of God's people go days, weeks, months—perhaps years—without really confessing their sin to God. No wonder so few are going on in revival.

And then there is the aspect of worship. Do we honestly worship God? Worship has been defined as a realization of the presence of God and a commitment of self to him. Worship is of the Spirit of God. This is why some of the most profound worship services are when you are alone with God. We cannot go on in revival without worshipping the Lord day by day.

If we are going on in revival we must continuously receive a cleansing. We cannot stay in a spirit of revival if we are unclean, and we cannot stay clean without consecration, separation, reading the Word of God, confession, and worship.

And we must exercise them daily!
If we are going on in revival we must:

CONSCIENTIOUSLY REVIEW
OUR CALLING

(Nehemiah 9:5-31)

Practically the entire ninth chapter of Nehemiah is devoted to the review of the callings and blessings of God on the Israelites. Conscientiously reviewing our calling, remembering who we are, where we have been, and where we are going are real keys to "going on in revival."

Our Position—Who We Are

If revival is to continue a constant reassessment of our position, our spiritual identity is necessary. The enemy's attacks will continue at the point of our personal identity. He will often ask, "Who do you think you are?" That is a good question, and we should have a ready answer. Nehemiah was only the cupbearer of the king, a civil servant. But he was more than that. He was one of God's chosen people. That outweighed everything else! He was a servant of the Most High God. However men saw him, Nehemiah saw himself as appointed and anointed for service.

Our constant identification with Christ in his death, burial, and resurrection is a necessity in going on with the Lord. We must be constantly aware of who we are in him.

Our Past—Where We Have Been

We cannot live in the past, but it is advantageous to look on the past every now and then. As the Israelites began to count their blessings they found them to be innumerable. Note the little connective "and" in verses 6 through 15. For instance:

> Thou alone are the Lord. Thou hast made the heavens, The heaven of heavens with all their host, The earth and all that is on it, The seas and all that is in them. Thou didst give life to all of them *And* the heavenly host bows down before Thee. Thou art the Lord God, Who chose Abram, *And* gave him the name Abraham. *And* Thou didst find his heart faithful before Thee, *And* didst make a covenant with him to give him the land of the Ca-

naanite, Of the Hittite and the Amorite, Of the Perizzite, the Jebusite, *and* the Girgashite—To give it to his descendants. *And* Thou has fulfilled Thy promise, For Thou art righteous. Thou didst see the affliction of our fathers in Egypt, *And* didst hear their cry by the Red Sea. Then Thou didst perform signs and wonders against Pharaoh, Against all his servants *and* all the people of his land; For Thou didst know that they acted arrogantly toward them, *And* didst make a name for Thyself as it is this day. *And* Thou didst divide the sea before them, So they passed through the midst of the sea on dry ground; *And* their pursers Thou didst hurl into the depths, Like a stone into raging waters. *And* with a pillar of cloud Thou didst lead them by day. *And* with a pillar of fire by night To light for them the way In which they were to go. Then Thou didst come down on Mount Sinai, *And* didst speak with them from heaven; Thou didst speak with them just ordinances and true laws, Good statues and commandments.

So Thou didst make known to them
Thy holy sabbath, *And* didst lay
down for them commandments,
statues, *and* laws, Through Thy servant Moses. Thou didst provide
bread from heaven for them for their
hunger, Thou didst bring forth water
from a rock for them for their thirst
And Thou didst tell them to enter in
order to possess The Land which
Thou didst swear to give them.
(9:6-15).

What a conscientious review of their calling! Remember, these experiences moti-
vated them to go on with God.

Our Potential—Where We Are Going

In all of this review, after looking inward
to review our position, and backward to
review our past, we now look forward to
view our potential. We are on a journey.
Much of our needless suffering results
from mistaking the journey for the destination. The goal of Nehemiah's heart was not
the height of a wall or the width of a
gate—but the glory of God. That is our
destination.

I have found this to be so true in my own
life. From time to time Satan tempts me to

give up, not to go on with God, to refrain from going on in revival! When this happens to you, I challenge you: begin to review your calling conscientiously. Begin to let those blessed memories of bygone days flow through your heart and mind. The day when you met Jesus. The day when you totally surrendered your life to him. The day when he answered that specific prayer. The day he blessed you with that special blessing. The day he reached down and comforted you as only he can. Oh, to review where we have been and to think about where we are going! It is good medicine in going on in revival.

If you are serious with God about going on in revival, when you are attacked by the devil, remember to review your calling. While we must never rest on yesterday's blessings, recounting them can be good medicine to spur us on. Many in the Bible have done this. What about you? Tempted to give up? Tempted to go along with the crowd? Tempted to stay out of revival? Stop! And conscientiously review your calling.

And finally, if we are going on in revival we must:

CONSTANTLY RENEW
OUR COMMITMENT

(Nehemiah 9:32-38)

Do you see the result of reviewing your calling? "Now, therefore, our God, the great, the mighty, and the awesome God, who dost keep covenant and lovingkindness, Do not let all the hardship seem insignificant before Thee, Which has come upon us, our kings, our princes, our priests, our prophets, our fathers, and on all Thy people" (9:32). After conscientiously reviewing their calling the Israelites renewed their commitment with God. It is important to note that we must constantly renew our commitment. Yesterday's commitment will not suffice for today! The children of Israel found this to be true at Ai! As you recall they had just won the decisive battle at Jericho. They began to think that *they* had won the victory instead of God. And they attacked Ai, a much smaller city not nearly as well-fortified. Therefore they took only a few men and suffered an amazing defeat having thirty-six of their men slain, all because they thought yesterday's commitment would suffice for today. If we are going on in revival we must constantly renew our commitment—day by day.

This commitment, our covenant with God, is discussed in chapter ten of Nehemiah. It involves renewing the commitment of the home life.

Now the rest of the people, the priests, the Levites, the gate keepers, the singers, the temple servants, and all those who had separated themselves from the peoples of the lands to the law of God, their wives, their sons and their daughters, all those who had knowledge and understanding, are joining with their kinsmen, their nobles, and are taking on themselves a curse and an oath to walk in God's law, which was given through Moses, God's servant, and to keep and to observe all the commandments of God our Lord, and His ordinances and His statutes; and that we will not give our daughters to the peoples of the land or take their daughters for our sons (10:28-30).

Many family altars are in desperate need

of repair today. It is the breakdown of America. A renewed commitment to God will always affect our home life. Not only that, it affects our social life. For the Israelites, a clear line of separation, as far as friendships were concerned, was apparent. Many a person has ended up where he never intended because he started running around with the wrong people. And this renewed commitment not only will affect our home life and our social life, but verse 39 tells us it affects our church life. "For the sons of Israel and the sons of Levi shall bring the contribution of the grain, the new wine and the oil, to the chambers; there are the utensils of the sanctuary, the priests who are ministering, the gatekeepers, and the singers. "Thus we will not neglect the house of our God" (Nehemiah 10:39). When revival comes we will not fail to attend the house of God. We will carry on with a ministry of attendance in the church of the living God.

. How long has it been since you renewed that commitment you made so long ago? If it was yesterday that will not get it. It's no wonder that in our day so few are going on with God in revival. Simply talking about how it used to be, about the good, old days of the past. If we are going to go on today we must constantly renew our commitment.

The theme of Nehemiah, when revival comes, has been so apparent through these pages. I trust many have seen the need, and have entered into revival in their own hearts. The question now is this—are you going on . . . in revival?

If so, I challenge you to conscientiously receive a cleansing—through consecration, separation, Bible study, confession, and worship. And when the going gets a little rough, when the devil makes his attack, when friends let you down, I challenge you to conscientiously review your calling. Remember what the Lord has done for you. Count your blessings. And then day by day constantly renew your commitment.

Coming now to Thee, O Christ my Lord,
Trusting only in Thy precious Word,
Let my humble prayer to Thee be heard,
And send a great revival in my soul.

Send the Holy Spirit now within,
Burning out the dross and guilt of
sin;
Let Thy mighty works of grace
begin,
Oh, send a great revival in my
soul.

Send a great revival in my soul,
Send a great revival in my soul,
Let the Holy Spirit come and take
control,
And send a great revival in my
soul. *

May God grant us the supernatural
power to . . . go on in revival!

A CHURCH MEMBER TRANSFORMED!

Herb was a paragon of faithfulness to his church. He was flawlessly moral and enjoyed total respect among the members of the church.

When revival comes, people begin to see themselves as God sees them. When that happened to Herb, he was shocked! He called his pastor and asked for an appointment. The pastor was surprised to hear what came out of Herb's mouth.

He heard this man, who was as faithful as any member in the church, confess that he had not slept much at all for more than two weeks. The reason? He knew himself to be a lost sinner who would go to hell if he died. In a little while this church member was ushered into the kingdom of God!

Too long, in too many minds, church

membership has been equated with salvation. As spiritual awakening comes to a
congregation, those with a surface commitment to the terms of the Gospel come to
find that their relationship must be with
Jesus Christ himself.

Lost church members form a formidable
barrier to revival. But when revival comes,
folks with joy draw water from the wells of
salvation. It always happens . . . when
revival comes!

Chapter 8

NEHEMIAH, MOSES, AND FLORIDA IN THE EIGHTIES

Nehemiah, Moses, And Florida In the Eighties

The question should be immediate, "What do Nehemiah, Moses, and Florida, 1980, have in common?" Admittedly, they are widely separated in chronology, as well as geography. But God has a way of bringing widely separated entities together. That is precisely what happened during the preparation of the manuscript for this book.

Allow me to recall a time recently when God confirmed in my heart the promise of revival in America. I was in a doctor's office in Atlanta, Georgia, and the Lord began speaking to my heart. I had prayed several days before that God would simply underline in my heart his promise of revival. I knew that this moment in Atlanta was God's chosen time for the answer to that prayer. I joyously tucked that promise away in my heart.

About six months later, the Lord awakened me early in the morning. I was refreshed, rested, and ready to listen to him. In my heart, he began to speak with me about the economic situation in America and throughout the world. I was impressed that I was receiving a new mandate to speak on the principles of God's economy wherever I was to be for the next months. Had I thought about it, I would have wondered about the connection between the promise of revival and the mandate to preach on God's principles of economy.

It was at this point that Florida came into focus. One of my first engagements after that early morning meeting with the Lord was in the First Baptist Church of Fort Lauderdale, Florida. As providence would have it, the pastor had been preaching from the book of Exodus. This is where Moses is highlighted.

In preaching through Exodus, particular anointing had been experienced when the pastor reached chapter thirty-five of that book. This is the chapter which records the command of the Lord to Moses to "take ye from among you an offering unto the Lord" (Ex. 35:5). The message aroused an immediate challenge among the people, and the idea was born to take a twentieth-century "Exodus Offering."

And exactly what is an Exodus Offering? I suppose that it was an offering which could be described as being a replica of that phenomenal offering taken by Moses in the wilderness. The equivalent of millions of dollars was raised in a few brief days in the wilderness for the construction of the tabernacle, the moveable tent which was to be the dwelling-place for God among his people.

Is it possible to imagine that a feat akin to that could be accomplished in the twentieth century? There was no committee, no goal, no pre-campaign study to determine the giving potential. There were no advance or challenge gifts sought. There were no glossy four-color brochures printed. In these several characteristics, the offering in the wilderness and the offering in Florida were similiar.

Someone suggested that stickers be printed and distributed which read plainly:

LORD, DO IT AGAIN

Exodus 36:3-7

In that passage the results of that offering in the wilderness were assessed. There was enough and more!

In Florida there was no torrid campaign schedule. In fact, there was no campaign. There was no emphasis on the amount of the need. This was to be a God-directed offering with people hearing from God regarding the amount and nature of their offering. For two months the people were challenged to fast and pray every Friday about the offering.

Again, as providence would plan it, I was to begin a meeting in the church on the very day the offering would be taken. The pastor and I had discussed no figures, and there was no set goal published or discussed with the church. One month and one day before the day of the offering, the Lord impressed me to believe him for a certain amount. I wrote that figure in my prayer book of requests. The pastor was impressed with a figure for the offering on that day of several thousand dollars short of my figure. He later found out that the amount that separated our figures had already been given without his prior knowledge! Thus our figures were exactly the same!

The day came and before the midnight

hour arrived, over $250,000 in cash and valuables had been given by the people of God in the First Baptist Church of Fort Lauderdale. Myriads of stories are coming from that offering of stunning disclosures from the Lord of gifts he wanted made. But each of those stories is obsolete upon its telling. The reason for that is: even before it is told another event in an unending chain reaction of events is taking place. In the weeks that followed, even as the deadline for the finishing of this manuscript came, awesome stories were gathering around the lives of those who entered into that offering.

And where does Nehemiah find an entrance into this story? Here in the book you hold in your hand, of course! It is probably obvious by now that the one word which fits all three stories, the one quality in common between Moses, Nehemiah, and Florida, is revival . . . a revival in which *givingness* is the key which unlocks the mysteries of the manifested presence of God.

The parts of the puzzle were coming together for me. The principal hindrance to the advance of the kingdom of God is greed. It is the chief obstacle to heaven-sent revival. In the case of Moses in Exodus, the people had experienced the moving of God among them to make their minds willing and their spirits stirred. They entered into spontaneous giving, and the result was nothing short of miraculous.

When one man, Nehemiah, was willing to give—give of himself, his time, his resources, his influence, and even his life, if necessary—revival came to a city in reproach. The people took heart, had a mind to work, and rebuilt ruined walls and reconstructed burned gates. And revival came to Nehemiah's day!

And why not in century twenty? And wherever I have been to lift up the message of the Bible regarding God's glorious plan of economy, which keys in on godly givingness, I have seen mercy drops fall from heaven. It seems that when the back of greed is broken, the human spirit soars into regions of unselfishness. God's Spirit takes over. God moves into man's affairs with his limitless resources. The results are more than amazing—they are, humanly speaking, unbelievable!

While men think of money, God thinks of men. It is not money God is after—it is people. The issue in all three cases here discussed is not how much, or even what kind, but that folks have heard from God, clearly and distinctly, and have heeded him. And this has given him cause to step into our situation.

There is a mounting crisis in world economy. Every economic prognosticator, almost without exception, is preaching doom. Every American has had his attention called for again and again in magazines, periodicals, and media news concerning the economy. It is the prime thorn in presidential flesh. Mounting interest rates, double-digit inflation, dollar devaluation, and threatened recession are howling like wolves at the nation's door.

Could it be that, at this very point, God is seeking to speak to us? Could the very point of pressure be the next point of revival possibilities? Could it be that God is bringing us as churches and individuals to the end of our resources so we might experience the beginning of heavenly resources? May the challenge from Nehemiah prove to be a personal one for you. May the experience from Exodus 35 and 36 send to your heart the issue which faces every one of us . . . to what extent are we willing to go with God in order that he may release his power upon the earth?

Paul makes an intriguing statement in 2 Corinthians 9:7. ''For God loveth a cheerful giver." The word in Greek is best identified with the English word "hilarious." Hilarious giving may prove to be one of the major gates through which revival comes to the people of God. I believe it's safe to say that there can be no continuous revival without hilarious giving. And I fear no contradiction: wherever there is hilarious giving there will soon be revival!

The whole focus of the issue of revival, of this volume, of your life, dear reader, comes to this point. Will you, in the name of Jesus Christ, who gave his all for you, give your all to him, and ask him to make you an agent of revival?

Would you right now consider the four following suggestions?

1. Transfer everything you have, everything you are, and everything you will ever have to the ownership of God.

2. Reckon on God as your sole resource from now on.

3. Ask God to initiate and orchestrate a giving program in your life founded on his riches and resourcefulness.

4. Ask God right now what he would

have you do to demonstrate your willingness to walk into spiritual reality.

Listen to the still, small voice of God and simply do as you are told.

This is the end of a volume. It can be the beginning of a victorious walk with God as you experience what happens . . . *when revival comes!*